A JUNGIAN PSYCHOLOGY
RESOURCE GUIDE

BOOKS BY JAMES AND TYRA ARRAJ:

A TOOL FOR UNDERSTANDING
HUMAN DIFFERENCES
How To Discover and Develop Your Type
According to Dr. C.G. Jung and Dr. William Sheldon
(Out of Print)

ST. JOHN OF THE CROSS AND DR. C.G. JUNG
Christian Mysticism in the Light of
Jungian Psychology

THE TREASURES OF SIMPLE LIVING
A Family's Search for a Simpler and
More Meaningful Life in the Middle of a Forest

A JUNGIAN PSYCHOLOGY RESOURCE GUIDE

Forthcoming:

TRACKING THE ELUSIVE HUMAN
A Guide to C.G. Jung's Psychological Types,
W.H. Sheldon's Body Types
and Their Integration

A JUNGIAN PSYCHOLOGY RESOURCE GUIDE

**LOCAL AND PROFESSIONAL GROUPS
PSYCHOLOGICAL TYPES
CONFERENCES
PERIODICALS • PUBLISHERS
MAIL ORDER BOOK SOURCES
LIBRARIES AND
BIBLIOGRAPHICAL TOOLS
BASIC READING LIST AND FILMS
JUNGIAN ANALYSIS
TRAINING PROGRAMS**

COMPILED BY
JAMES AND TYRA ARRAJ
TOOLS FOR INNER GROWTH

Printed in the United States of America.

For ordering information on this and other titles see
the back pages or write:
Tools for Inner Growth
Box 520
Chiloquin, OR 97624

This book is printed on acid free paper.

Library of Congress Cataloging-in-Publication Data

A Jungian psychology resource guide.

    Includes index.
    1. Psychology--Information services. 2. Jung, C. G.
(Carl Gustav), 1875-1961--Information services.
I. Arraj, Jim. II. Arraj, Tyra.
BF76.72.J86 1987   150.19'54   87-25557
ISBN 0-914073-05-2 (alk. paper)

CONTENTS

INTRODUCTION

We are happy to introduce this first edition of **A Jungian Psychology Resource Guide.** The simple fact of its existence more than 25 years after Jung's death testifies to the enduring qualities of his work, which is spreading all over the world and significantly, not only by way of professional groups, but through grass-roots organizations as well.

A glance at the **Contents** will indicate the major divisions of the **Guide.** There is some inevitable overlapping of categories which can be sorted out by examining the index at the back of the book. In addition to Jungian organizations, we have listed some Jungian-oriented organizations, that is, resources that are not directly Jungian, but are of interest to a Jungian audience.

Sources

Quotation marks in a listing indicates a description coming from the group's own literature or correspondence sent to us. In some cases these descriptions have been lightly edited.

The examples given of recent lectures, courses, books, etc., beyond illustrating the activities of a particular group, can have the cumulative effect of providing us with a glimpse into interests and preoccupations of the current world of Jungian psychology.

Improving This Guide

In the rapidly growing and fluid world of Jungian psychology we are bound to have missed organizations that should have been included or have information that needs to be updated or is simply incorrect. Share your knowledge with us. Let us know of organizations you feel ought to be included or corrections that should be made.

Acknowledgements

We would like to thank the many people who responded to our inquiries. We would also like to thank Joan Alpert, Librarian of the C.G. Jung Institute, San Francisco, for her help and encouragement, and for providing an updated basic reading list.

BASIC QUESTIONS
AND WHERE TO FIND THE ANSWERS

Who was C.G. Jung? Read his autobiographical **Memories, Dreams, Reflections** and the biographies that have appeared about him. (See Chapter 9)

What did he say? Examine his **Collected Works,** his published letters and seminars. (#9)

How can I get a real picture of what he was like? See films. (#9)

How can I get an idea of books and articles that exist about Jung's psychology? See Libraries and Bibliographical Tools (#8) and Basic Reading List. (#9)

Where can I get books on Jungian psychology? Your local bookstore can order any book in print. See, in addition, Jungian book publishers (#6) and Mail-Order book sources. (#7)

Where do I look when starting research on a topic in Jungian psychology? See Libraries and Bibliographical Tools. (#8)

Where can I find a Jungian analyst? Contact your nearest Jungian professional group (#1 & 2) or see the IAAP membership directory. (#10)

Where can I meet people interested in Jung? See Local Groups. (#1 & 2)

What periodicals exist in Jungian psychology or with Jungian-oriented material? See Periodicals. (#5)

What is Jungian Analysis like? See Jungian Analysis and Training Programs. (#10)

What does it take to become a Jungian analyst? See Jungian Analysis and Training Programs. (#10)

How can I find the up-to-date programs of U.S. local and professional groups? See Centerpoint's **In Touch** (#1)

How can I keep track of the activities of foreign professional groups? See the IAAP **Newsletter.** (#10)

1 LOCAL AND PROFESSIONAL GROUPS IN THE UNITED STATES AND CANADA

ALABAMA

Friends of Jung-South
4125 Abingdon Lane
Birmingham, AL 35243

"**Friends of Jung-South,** the pioneer Jungian group in the southeast, was incorporated on December 28, 1981, its primary purpose being to further the development of Jungian Psychology and related fields in the United States, and primarily but not exclusively the southern geographical portion thereof, by virtue of organizing, sponsoring and/or funding lectures, seminars, conferences and the like dealing with Jungian Psychology and related fields and to otherwise promote understanding and utilization, both clinical and academic, of Jungian Psychology.

Membership is open to anyone. Members receive a thoughtful quarterly newsletter which keeps them abreast of Jungian and related events locally and internationally, as well as of current books and thinking.

In its six years, **Friends of Jung-South** has sponsored workshops and seminars featuring outstanding Jungian analysts and writers and, from its original membership from all over the area, has spawned more than a half-dozen other active Jungian organizations.

The City of Birmingham, which had no Jungian analysts in 1981, now has three; in 1985 the Interregional Society of Jungian Analysts met here, and at the University of Alabama at Birmingham, ongoing Jungian study is available. Numerous Jungian counselors are now found in widely varied human development institutions."

Phoenix Friends of C.G. Jung
P.O. Box 9387
Scottsdale, AZ 85252
(602) 948-3244 or 947-9858

"We were organized in May of 1984 after attending a series of six lectures entitled, "Calling the Friends of Jung", given by Mary Palombo at the Franciscan Renewal Center in Scottsdale.

Our purpose as stated in our Article of Incorporation is "to meet as a society of people sharing a common interest in the analytical psychology of Carl G. Jung, to provide activities for the growth of this interest, and to encourage the individuation process." Membership is open to all who share this interest.

We offer a calendar of events newsletter in the spring and the fall, we sell books and tapes at our lectures, and we hope to start a library in the near future.

We have several groups throughout the Valley meeting in Centerpoint studies."

Some recent lectures:

"Experience in Self Expression" by Hank Lukas.

"Through the Belly of the Whale" by John Sanford.

Southern Arizona Friends of C.G. Jung
4940 Calle Barril
Tucson, AZ 85718
(602) 299-6352 or 326-6298

"**Southern Arizona Friends of C.G. Jung** was founded in 1982 by a group of four women who recognized the growing interest in the analytical psychology of C.G. Jung and who sought to provide activities for the growth of this interest.

We sponsor workshops, lectures, and discussion groups which pertain to Jungian psychology for members and the general public. For these workshops and lectures Jungian analysts and other experts in the field, both from Tucson and from other parts of the country, are brought in to present programs in their particular areas of interest or expertise.

Also, discussion groups are organized within the membership on subjects pertaining to Jungian psychology. A particular publication or movie may be the focus or a particular aspect of Jungian psychology. Membership is open to any interested person. Brochures of our programs and newsletters are published twice a year."

CALIFORNIA

The Psychotherapy Institute
2320 Channing Way
Berkeley, CA 94704

The C.G. Jung Club of Claremont
c/o Claremont Psychological Services, Inc.
4353 North Towne Avenue
Claremont, CA 91711
(714) 624-4414

"Our group's aim is to unite individuals with an interest in the work of C.G. Jung and to share how his ideas are used in the fields of psychology, art, religion, education, etc. Members receive a quarterly newsletter describing monthly lectures and access to growth activities. The membership fee enables members to attend these meetings free of charge and they may attend our annual seminar at a reduced rate."

C.G. Jung Institute of Los Angeles
Analytical Psychology Club of Los Angeles
Society of Jungian Analysts of Southern
   California - Los Angeles
10349 West Pico Boulevard
Los Angeles, CA 90064
(213) 556-1193

The C.G. Jung Institute of Los Angeles is a non-profit, educational organization which provides:
   training for persons interested in becoming certified Jungian analysts (see #10) and sponsors educational and research programs for Jungian analysts and other professionals,
   the Kieffer E. Frantz Clinic, a low-fee clinic and referral service
   the Hilde Kirsch Children's Center, which offers therapy for children
   and publishes the semi-annual journal **Psychological Perspectives** (see #5)
   the Max and Lore Zeller Library (see #8) and the C.G. Jung Bookstore (see #7)
   ARAS: Archive for Research in Archetypal Symbolism. It is a unique collection of pictures and scholarly material devoted to the study of symbolic imagery. (see #8)
   Friends of ARAS, a support group designed to further research into cultures not yet included in the collection, and which invites your participation.
   public lecture series and seminars held several times each year. Recent lectures:
   "Male Mid-Life: A Time of Unfolding" by Richard Friedman.
   "The New Psychobiology of Mind-Body Healing", an all day conference.

Central Coast Jung Society
1566 Ninth Street
Los Osos, CA 93402
(805) 528-4121

The **Central Coast Jung Society** "started in 1981 with a small group of participants interested in Jung who met on a monthly basis on Sunday evenings for a pot luck dinner and discussions of Jungian topics.

Starting this year we have initiated a series of lectures on Wednesday evenings once a month. We anticipate continuing this next autumn.

Lectures are open to the general public. So far there are no membership dues.

We offer the sale of books by our catalog through publishers specializing in Jungian materials.

Monterey Peninsula Friends of C.G. Jung
853 Pacific Street
Monterey, CA 93940
(408) 649-8809

"We are an informal organization of some 550 people who meet fairly regularly to share an enthusiasm for Jung's seminal ideas. Small groups hold living room meetings once or twice a month. Currently there are groups which meet whose focus of discussion is dream sharing, book reading (**Inner World of Choice** by Wickes), dreambody-processwork (using Arnold Mindell's books), typology, and seven tasks of later life.

There are no membership requirements, for there is no membership as such. The public is invited to all our events. We announce events through an occasional memorandum. We have a small circulating library.

Recent lectures:

"The Body in Drawings, Movements, and Sound" by Peter Harding.

"The Seven Tasks of Later Life" by Joseph Pagano.

C.G. Jung Club of Orange County
P.O. Box 1812
Orange, CA 92668
(714) 964-5741

"The **C.G. Jung Club of Orange County** began in 1973. The purpose of this organization is to educate the general public in their interest and knowledge of Jungian Psychology. Membership is open to anyone who genuinely desires to support the purpose of the association.

Our organization publishes a newsletter 2-3 times a year in addition to various supplementary material on programs, meetings, and so forth. There are several programs throughout the year focusing on Jungian related topics. Each spring we sponsor an annual Jungian conference which is a day-long event usually featuring a keynote speaker in the morning and selected workshops in the afternoon. The last conference was "The Eros Connection: Finding Love and Intimacy in Our Times".

We support an extensive library of Jungian material and books, which is readily available to the members."

The Friends of Jung
3525 Front Street
San Diego, CA 92103-0360
(619) 291-JUNG

"After careful planning, **The Friends of Jung** was formally organized in April, 1976, to advance the growth of analytical psychology among its members and in San Diego County through a variety of ways and to maintain contact with similar organizations throughout the United States and the world."

It has a book service, library, lectures and workshops. A large collection of tapes for sale includes:

"Basque Mysticism" by Angeles Arrien

"The Vision Quest Among Native Americans" by Guilford Dudley
"Hasidic Tales and Jungian Psychology: A Dialogue" by Maurice Friedman
"Raja Yoga and Jung's Psychology" by Thomas Parker

Society of Jungian Analysts of San Diego
c/o Verda Heisler
3304 Brant Street
San Diego, CA 92103
(619) 298-1135

The **Society of Jungian Analysts of San Diego** has a training program.

C.G. Jung Institute of San Francisco
Society of Jungian Analysts of Northern
California - San Francisco
2040 Gough Street
San Francisco, CA 94109
(415) 771-8055

"The **C.G. Jung Institute of San Francisco** was formed in 1964 to foster and develop Carl Jung's theories and approaches and to make these available to the interested public. The **Institute** was created by the **Society of Jungian Analysts of Northern California,** a body of professionals who had joined together to support and enhance their mutual interests and professional development and to train new Jungian analysts."
For the Analyst Training Program, see #10.
"The **James Goodrich Whitney Clinic** was named in honor of one of the charter members of the **Institute,** a man who was most active in the early development both of the **Institute** and the **Clinic.** Since its inception, the purpose of the Clinic has been to provide Jungian analysis or Jungian-oriented psycho-

therapy which is individual, unhurried, and in-depth, to applicants who are unable to afford regular or even moderately reduced fees.

The **Institute** offers programs for experienced psychotherapists who wish to deepen and expand their understanding of Jungian theory and practice. Seminar programs, offered during the fall and spring, consist of eight to ten weekly evening sessions, with groups usually limited to twenty people."

Recent Seminars for Professionals:

"Psychologies of Other Cultures" by Bruce Scotton

"Couples Counseling" by Seymour Radin

The **Institute's** public seminars, lectures, evening courses and symposia offer original work by eminent practitioners, scholars and artists in the fields of Jungian psychology and its correlative disciplines.

Recent public lectures and seminars:

"Individuation in the Face of Collective Mentality" by Dieter Baumann

"Psychological Types" by John Beebe and Jane Wheelwright

"The Jungian Challenge to Modern Christianity: From Spiritual Perfection to Psychological Wholeness" by Murray Stein, John P. Dourley, Joan Chamberlain Engelsman, Alan Jones and Donald P. Sandner.

For **ARAS** (The Archive for Research in Archetypal Symbolism) see #8.

For **The Virginia Allan Detloff Library** see #8.

For **The Library Journal** see #8.

Books published by the **Institute** are distributed through **Spring** and **Sigo** (see #6). They include:

St. George and the Dandelion: 40 Years of Practice as a Jungian Analyst by Joseph B. Wheelwright

Sandplay Studies, an anthology.

Monographs, distributed direct by the **Institute,** include:

"The Imitation of Jung: An Exploration of the Meaning of "Jungian"", by R. James Yandell

"Women and Men" by Jane Wheelwright

The **Institute** offers tapes, such as:
"Science, Religion & Jung: Toward a Post-Freudian Synthesis" by James Hall
"Dis-Ease & Self-Healing" by Sam Keen
Contact Peggy Sugars, P.O. Box 609, Fairfax, CA 94930 for ordering information.
The **Institute** also publishes the Gray-Wheelwrights Jungian Type Survey Test. (see #3)

Analytical Psychology Club of San Francisco
2411 Octavia Street
San Francisco, 94109

"The purpose of the **Club** is to promote the study and discussion of Analytical Psychology and related subjects, and to provide an opportunity for companionship among those who have experienced Jungian analysis.
Meetings are held regularly from fall through spring, usually on the second Friday evening of the month, at a central location in San Francisco. The meetings vary in subject matter, but most programs relate directly to Analytical Psychology. Following the meetings members and guests are invited to share informally with each other.
The **Club** maintains a library of over 3,000 items (books, periodicals, papers, tapes, etc.) to which additions are continuously made. Use of the Library is encouraged.
The **Club** was founded in 1940 by Dr. Elizabeth Whitney, Dr. Lucille Elliot, and Dr. and Mrs. Joseph Wheelwright.
Membership consists of (1) people having had at least 100 hours of analysis and who are considered qualified for membership by a recommending analyst, (2) members of the **International Association for Analytical Psychology** and trainees in the control stage in the **C.G. Jung Institute of San Francisco,** and (3) members in good standing in other Analytical

Psychology Clubs that have membership standards similar to those of the **APC** of San Francisco.

The **Club** has published **C.G. Jung, Emma Jung and Toni Wolff,** edited by Ferne Jensen.

Guild for Psychological Studies
2230 Divisadero Street
San Francisco, CA 94115
(415) 931-0647
and
Four Springs
14598 Sheveland Road
Middletown, CA 95461

"**The Guild for Psychological Studies** has for over 40 years functioned to face the problems of each decade. Today its goal seems more urgent than ever before.

The general purpose of the **Guild** is to assist individuals in their search for a fuller experience and expression of life in the day-to-day situation and in its relationship to the larger meaning and purpose of life on this planet. Seminars are primarily concerned with helping each participant to grow in the understanding of what it means to be a value-centered choice-maker in today's world, to find a religious and psychological ground of being from which choices can be made, and to take action on those insights.

Located on 300 forested acres, 85 miles north of San Francisco, Four Springs is the center for this work of individual transformation. In the 1500 foot high hills of Lake County, California the site provides a main lodge, seminar room, meditation room, library, art room, cabins, swimming pool, grape arbor, orchards and trails. Long seminars, study weeks and weekends constitute a year-round program. In addition, seminars, lectures, training and research are sponsored in San Francisco. San Francisco events and weekend seminars at Four Springs are listed in

the **Winter-Spring** and in the **Fall-Winter** Programs."
Representative programs:
"A Study of the Records of the Life of Jesus"
"By the Holy Spirit Beguiled"
"Then Why Did We Marry?"
"Why Were We Born? Why Do We Suffer?"
Weekend seminars are offered regularly in Portland, OR, Denver, CO, Claremont, CA and Seattle, WA.

Human Relations Institute
5200 Hollister Avenue
Santa Barbara, CA 93111
(805) 967-4557

Recent offerings:
"Animals and Dreams", a seminar series exploring the ecology of the psyche including:
"Henry David Thoreau and the Secret Life Within" by Robert Bly
"Establishing Special Respect for the Animals that Come to Us in the Night" by James Hillman
"Learning the Craft of Dream Work" by Stephen Aizenstat.
This seminar series was presented in conjunction with the **Human Relations Institute's** M.A. Degree Program in Counseling Psychology, with degree specialization in Depth Psychology.
The interdisciplinary course work of the program includes: Jung's depth psychology, Freud's depth psychology, clinical methodologies, marriage and family therapies, dream interpretation, alchemical studies, myth and literature, ancient healing rites and archetypal psychology. (partial listing)
The **Institute** also presents:
The Fourth Annual Imagination of Greece Conference, "Descending with Orpheus", features Christine Downing.

University of California Extension
Santa Cruz, CA 95064
(408) 429-2971

Courses include:
"Practicum in Sandplay", a continuing training for professionals, by Estelle Weinrib and Katherine Bradway.
"Sacred Earth", a study tour to the southwest, by Edith Sullwold.
"Process-Oriented Psychology" by Arnold Mindell.
"Sandplay in Switzerland", a three week training program, with Dora Kalff.

COLORADO

Julie Penrose Center
1661 Mesa Avenue
Colorado Springs, CO 80906-2998
(303) 632-2451

C.G. Jung Educational and Research Center
930 Logan Street
Denver, CO 80203
(303) 831-9209

"**The C.G. Jung Educational and Research Center, Inc.** provides a (1) training of the Jungian Analysts, (2) a curriculum program for professional people in the study of the psychology of C.G. Jung, and (3) a program of classes which are open to the public. These classes are related to many areas of Jungian psychology. We also invite Jungian Analysts from other parts of the country and from Europe to give lectures and workshops for us.
The analyst training program is carried out under the auspices of the **Inter-Regional Society of Jungian Analysts** of which we are a member training center.
Our goal is to continue the study of the psycho-

logy of C.G. Jung and to bring his ideas before those people interested in them while at the same time expanding our own interest and knowledge."

The C.G. Jung Society of Colorado
Dept. of Religious Studies
University of Denver
Denver, CO 80208
(303) 871-2740-1
    and
c/o Mrs. Hawley
2135 S. Columbine
Denver, CO 80210

"The aim of our organization is to promote interest in Jungian thought and provide lectures related to Jung's thought. We were organized in January 1976 and are co-sponsored by the Religious Studies Department at the University of Denver. Our lecture series occurs during the academic year.
    Recent examples:
    "The Ravaged Groom" by Marion Woodman
    "The "Iron John" Quality of Masculinity: Rough, Fierce, Wild" by Eugene Monick.

CONNECTICUT

Connecticut Association for Jungian Psychology
94 State Street
Guilford, CT 06437
(203) 228-9927 or 453-0437

The Country Place
Box 668
Litchfield, CT 06759
(203) 567-8763

The Country Place is a Jungian based long-term treatment center for emotionally disturbed young adults, 18 years or older.

Temenos Institute, Inc.
29 East Main Street
Westport, CT 06880
(203) 227-4388

The **Institute** offers a certificate program in Humanistic/Transpersonal Psychology with option for a Masters Degree.

DELAWARE

Round Table Associates
42 Butternut Court
Valley Run, DE 19810
(302) 475-7916

DISTRICT OF COLUMBIA

Washington Society for Jungian Psychology
2948 Brandywine Street, NW
Washington, DC 20008
(301) 966-7414

"Our organization was started informally in the late 1970's, incorporated as the **C.G. Jung Working Group** in the early 1980's and changed the name to the **Washington Society for Jungian Psychology** in 1985. Since our beginning our aim has been to provide the community with opportunities to learn about the life and work of Carl Jung through lectures, workshops, small group sharing, and courses of study.
We inherited the personal library of the first Jungian analyst in Washington, Elinid Kotschnig, and we are in the process of preparing it for circulation. It is housed in Philanthropon House where Dr. Marguerite Fogel lives and works as a therapist. She has extended the use of her **C.G. Jung Library and In-**

formation Center to our members."

Inner Development Associates
5201 MacArthur Terrace NW
Washington, DC 20016
(202) 364-1075

Inner Development makes available the following materials:
Dreams and Spiritual Growth: A Judeo-Christian Approach to Dreamwork by Louis M. Savary, Patricia H. Berne and Strephon Williams, Paulist Press
Dreams and Spiritual Growth (video cassette) by Louis M. Savary and Patricia Berne, Paulist Press
Spiritual Growth Through Dreams (6 cassettes, 5 hours) with a study guide by Louis M. Savary, Credence Cassettes.

FLORIDA

Center for Applications of Psychological Type, Inc. (CAPT)
2720 N.W. 6th Street
Gainesville, FL 32609
(904) 375-0160

Workshops on types are being run across the country. See #3.

The C.G. Jung Society of Northeast Florida
c/o Hank Walters
1911 Landwood Street
Jacksonville, FL 32211
(904) 721-3499

"The C.G. Jung Society of Northeast Florida was established in January 1983 for the purpose of presenting information about analytical psychology in accordance with the theories and methodology originated by Jung.

The many facets of analytical psychology are explored through lectures, films, workshops, small study/discussion groups and conferences. Two major lectures are planned each year, and in the past have featured such well-known Jungian scholars as Thomas Kapacinskas, Murray Stein, and Marion Woodman. Monthly meetings feature speakers on a wide variety of subjects, and special workshops and study groups are offered throughout the year. At many activities, Continuing Education Units are available for mental health and medical professionals.

Membership in the Society is open to anyone with a personal or professional interest in exploring analytical psychology, and members receive the **C.G. Jung Society of Northeast Florida Newsletter.**"

Recent lectures:

"Mandalas: Maps of Inner Space" by Louis Woods

"Guided Imagery as a Tool for Active Imagination" by Barbara Ritch.

CASHEL
Center for Psychology and the Arts
818 North Federal Highway
Lake Worth, FL 33460

"The aim of **CASHEL** is to nurture and foster psychology and the arts at the grass-roots level. It was founded as a non-profit organization by Julia Brown and Charles Wright in 1979.

The membership requirements are a genuine interest and commitment to regular discussion meetings, plus fees.

Discussion meetings and supper are held monthly every second Sunday. Special events have been:

"Way of the Dream" film series

Ira Progoff's workshops

An annual newsletter summarizes meetings, events and items of interest. **CASHEL** has a growing library, and hosts, when possible, art exhibitions, poetry readings, Centerpoint series and Art Therapy Journal Series."

Florida Jung Group
P.O. Box 3804
West Palm Beach, FL 33402

GEORGIA

Epworth-by-the-Sea Conference Center
St. Simons Island, GA

For a Jungian-oriented conference held here, see #4.

HAWAII

C.G. Jung Center of Hawaii, Inc.
7844 Makaaoa Place
Honolulu, HI 96825
(808) 395-6157

ILLINOIS

C.G. Jung Institute of Chicago
Chicago Society of Jungian Analysts
550 Callan Avenue
Evanston, IL 60202
(312) 475-4848 or 273-3040

The **Institute** offers two distinct programs:
the Analyst Training Program, which is an extended course of study for qualified candidates leading to certification as a Jungian analyst (see #10)
the Public Education Program, which is open to all interested persons.
Recent lectures, workshops and courses include:
"Dream Imagery Constellated by the Analytic

Process"
"Archetypes and Personal History in the Development of the Personality"
"Psychological Aspects of Religious Experience"
"The Shadow and the Father" by Donald Sandner
"The Death of Christ and His Descent into the Underworld" by Marvin Acklin.
A recent conference was:
"Civilization in Transition: Jung's Challenge to Culture in Crisis"
"In addition to the educational programs, the **Institute** houses a reference library (see #8) and a full-service bookstore featuring titles in psychology, myth, folklore and fairy tales, religion and pastoral counseling, art, and much more. (see #7) We have films and videotapes available for rental, and an extensive library of audiotapes for sale or rental.
The **Institute** is a resource for both lay and professional persons. All individuals who are concerned with inner development and its practical application for themselves and others will find a supportive yet non-intrusive environment within the **Institute**."

Friends of Jung/Quad Cities
c/o Sally Vande Voort
1930 31st Street, A
Moline, IL 61265
(309) 762-0195

Recent lectures:
"Archetypes of Easter" by Robert Staes
"Goddesses in Everywoman" by Jean Bolen

C.G. Jung Club of Rockford
c/o 319 Reynolds Street
Rockford, IL 61103

INDIANA

Friends of Jung
c/o Dean Frantz
3831 Evergreen Lane
Fort Wayne, IN 46815
(219) 486-3555

"The **Friends of Jung** sponsor several public presentations each year. Presentations have included: John Sanford, Robert Johnson, Anthony Stevens, Anne Maguire, and Marion Woodman; a Jung Film Festival; and a Reader's Theater on the Freud-Jung Letters.

The usual format of public programs include a Friday night lecture on the subject under consideration, and an all day seminar on Saturday. The purpose of these presentations is to relate the basic ideas of Jung to the contemporary issues faced by individuals and the world."

They also publish **The Loggia,** their newsletter.

J. Gary Sparks
3333 C East 79th Street
Indianapolis, IN 46240
(317) 255-6421

IOWA

Iowa City Friends of C.G. Jung
1033 E. Washington
Iowa City, IA 55240
(319) 337-7542

KENTUCKY

The LAPIS Group (Louisville Area Psychological Insights Study Group)
c/o Kell Julliard
928 Lydia Street
Louisville, KY 40217
(502) 634-3081

"The **LAPIS Group** is a loosely organized grass-roots association of persons wanting to learn about Jung and exists primarily to sponsor workshops and courses."

LOUISIANA

Arcadiana Friends of Jung
c/o Sandy Green
#7 Eureka Plantation Road
Lafayette, LA 70508
(318) 233-5472

New Horizons Art Therapy and Counseling Center
113 West Convent Street
Lafayette, LA 70501
(318) 234-9924 or 235-1784

"**New Horizons** is dedicated to the idea of balanced learning and development. All programs and services are designed to result in a transformation of the student or client through acquiring new knowledge and skills and the integration of this new material into the person's daily living.

Programs and ongoing groups are involved in the study and practice of such modern psychologies as Transactional Analysis, Gestalt Therapy and Jungian psychology, as well as in personal growth systems and holistic health attitudes.

In addition, we offer a Training Course in Art Therapy and Counseling. We have available an extensive lending library, and we have ongoing group work in addition to our counseling services.

MAINE

Bowdoin College Jung Seminar
Prof. William D. Geoghegan
Bowdoin College

Department of Religion
Mass. Hall
Brunswick, ME 04011
(207) 725-3537

The **Bowdoin College Jung Seminar** will begin its seventh year in the fall of 1987. Intended primarily for Bowdoin students, it is also open to Faculty and Staff and to interested members of the general public, all without charge. Sponsored by the Bowdoin College Department of Religion, the co-founders and co-leaders of the seminar are William D. Geoghegan and Bruce A. Riegel.

The **Bowdoin College Jung Seminar** meets every Tuesday from 4-5:30 pm when classes are in session. Meetings usually consist of close reading and discussion of works by or about Jung; the analysis and interpretation of symbols of the unconscious in dreams and art works, such as plays, paintings or poems. The **Seminar** sponsors lectures by Jungian analysts, symposia and films.

Dr. Kenneth Silvestro
Bowdoin College
Computer Science Department
Adams Hall
Brunswick, ME 04011
(207) 725-3569

A recent weekend retreat:
"Addiction and Creativity" by Linda Leonard and Keith Chapman.

Dwinell & Hall
Birch Knolls
Cape Elizabeth, ME 04107
(207) 799-1024

They have a new workshop every month on "Introduction to the Myers-Briggs Type Indicator".

Inner Life Institute
RFD 3, Box 131 A
Ellsworth, ME 04605

MASSACHUSETTS

C.G. Jung Institute - Boston
New England Society of Jungian Analysts
266 Beacon Street
Boston, MA 02116
(617) 267-5984

"The Training Program offers courses for Candidates in Training and, where designated in individual announcements, to a limited number of auditors." (see #10) The **Institute** and the **New England Society of Jungian Analysts** sponsor a series of seminars, lectures and workshops for Candidates in Training, Jungian Analysts, and auditors.
They include:
"The Organ of Skin as the Mirror of Psyche" by Anne Maguire
"The Myth of Matriarchy and its Consequences on Jung's Theory" by Janet Spenser
"Stress and the Zenless, Dying Puer" by Jeffrey Satinover
The **Institute** has a library open to the public on weekdays 10-3. Borrowing privileges for trainees and analysts only. The **Institute** also has a bookstore with the same hours.

Friends of Jung in Boston
Jungian Art Therapy Network
c/o Ethne Gray

112 Chestnut Street
West Newton, MA 02165
(617) 332-0383

The **Friends of Jung in Boston** hold meetings monthly. Lectures and discussions are on topics related to the psychology of Carl Jung, and includes an archetypal and imaginal approach to issues affecting human growth and society. Membership is open to anyone interested in Jungian psychology.

Jungian Art Therapy Network has a newsletter, **IRIS,** and a bi-annual conference on Jungian Art Therapy, held at the University of New Mexico, Albuquerque, NM. Membership is open to all, particularly expressive therapists.

Entheos
P.O. Box 256
Lincoln, MA 01773
(617) 259-9609 or 861-8873

They have dream forums and workshops.

Interface
Box 299
230 Central Street
Newton, MA 02166
(617) 964-0500

A recent lecture:
"Other Lives, Other Selves" by Roger Woolger

Andover Newton Seminars
Andover Newton Theological School
210 Herrick Road
Newton Centre, MA 02159
(617) 964-1100

They are sponsoring a 3-week seminar called

"Advanced Studies in Jungian Thought and Experience", held at the **C.G. Jung Institute**, Zürich.

MICHIGAN

The Center for Jung Studies of Detroit
The Village Professional Building
17150 Kercheval Avenue
Grosse Pointe, MI 48230
(313) 881-7970

The **Center for Jung Studies of Detroit** offers courses, workshops and lectures. They include:
Course: "Introduction to Jungian Dream Work - Theory and Method" by JoAnne Isbey
Seminar: "Cultivating the Contemplative - A Way of Individuation" by Sister Christian Koontz
Workshop: "The Native American Medicine Wheel" by Bill and Jody Wahlberg
Workshop: Religion and Analytical Psychology - "Changing Leaves and Blossoms on the Stem of the Eternal Tree" by J. Gary Sparks.
"Membership is open to anyone who is interested in Jungian psychology. We have a reference library and a book store."

Northern Michigan Friends of Jung
P.O. Box 238
Harbor Springs, MI 49740
(616) 526-2436 or 526-2486

MINNESOTA

Minnesota Jung Association
2400 Stevens Avenue, South
Minneapolis, MN 55404
(612) 870-1459

"The **Minnesota Jung Association** is dedicated to

the exploration of the human psyche through the study, promotion, and practical application of the discoveries of Analytical Psychology. Following the tradition of the Swiss physician Carl Gustav Jung, the Association seeks to recognize and enhance the growth of the individual personality, conscious that the vitality of the human community is based upon the living authenticity of its members."

Activities and Services:

public lectures featuring local and visiting analysts, scholars, and artists

seminars and workshops

informal study groups

Elements, the bi-monthly newsletter

low-fee psychotherapy services

Analyst Training is supported by the **Minnesota Jung Association** through the affiliation of its analyst-members with the **Inter-Regional Society of Jungian Analysts**

The **Minnesota Jung Association Library**

MISSOURI

Friends of Jung of Greater Kansas City
P.O. Box 30094
Kansas City, MO 64112
(816) 474-8260

MONTANA

Montana Friends of C.G. Jung
1440 Mountain View
Missoula, MT 59802

"**The Montana Friends of C.G. Jung** came into existence formally with a meeting on June 6, 1986, having evolved from a dream workshop conducted by Phil Morton.

Our general aims are to promote Jungian workshops of various types (mask-making, mandalas, dream analysis, fairy tales, Centerpoint, etc.) The goal is to foster self-understanding through Jungian concepts."

A recent weekend lecture and workshop:

"The Artist's Pursuit of Perfection" by Anne Devore.

NEW HAMPSHIRE

The Centerpoint Foundation
33 Main Street, #302
Nashua, NH 03060
(603) 880-3020

The Centerpoint Foundation offers a variety of different programs and services "dedicated to helping people become more conscious of their inner and outer world."

In Touch is a newsletter published three times a year, which contains short articles and interviews, but is especially useful for listing the current programs of Jungian organizations all over the United States and Canada. If you need a way to keep current on what many of the organizations in this **Guide** are doing, **In Touch** is the best way to do it.

Centerpoint, conceived and designed by Elsom Eldridge and Chandler Brown in 1972, "is designed for people who feel their basic understandings are compatible with Jungian psychology and who seek an ongoing context in which to pursue their own inner journey." The foundation offers three different programs:

Questpoint, a beginner's course with nine sessions, each around 2 hours long. "No leaders are required, presentations are on cassette tapes, and each member receives a notebook containing full transcripts of the tapes."

"**Centerpoint** is designed for people who feel their

basic understandings are compatible with Jungian psychology and who seek an ongoing context in which to pursue their own inner journey. There are three "years" of **Centerpoint**, a "year" meaning eighteen sessions, each about 2 hours."

Vantage Point is a new series of short courses. "**Vantage Point's** reflections are from mythology, Jungian psychology and various religious traditions from the East and West; Jewish, Christian, Gnostic, etc."

Centerpoint offers a 10% discount of almost 100 books in the field of Jungian psychology. It also rents the BBC films "Face-to-Face", John Freeman's interview with Carl Jung, and "The Story of Carl Gustav Jung", narrated by Sir Laurens Van Der Post.

It also sponsors the annual conference **Harvest.** (see #4)

NEW JERSEY

Mid-Life Directions
45 Poe Avenue
Valisburg, NJ 07106
(201) 373-6108

Mid-Life Directions is a ministry to people from 35 to 65+. It offers workshops, retreats and seminars, and trains people to give **Mid-Life Direction Workshops.** It was founded in 1978 by Anne Brennan and Janice Brewi "to offer workshops for the personal and spiritual growth of mid-life adults" in line with Jung's complaint that people were "wholly unprepared to embark on the second half of life". They wrote:

Mid-Life Psychological and Spiritual Perspectives
Mid-Life Praying and Playing Sources of New Dynamism

A recent retreat-workshop was "designed to prepare ministers to facilitate the personal and spiritual growth of mid-life adults through the mid-life directions process." It includes retreat, workshop and in-depth introduction to Jungian psychology.

NEW MEXICO

The Inter-Regional Society of Jungian Analysts
1520 Cerro Gordo
Santa Fe, NM 87501
(505) 982-3716 or 982-5693

"The Inter-Regional Society of Jungian Analysts is a training institute authorized by the **International Association of Analytical Psychology** to train certified Jungian analysts. **The Inter-Regional Society** presently has training branches in Denver, Santa Fe, Houston, Dallas, Austin, Minneapolis/St. Paul, Montreal, Quebec City, Virginia Beach, St. Louis, Memphis and Birmingham."
Some recent lectures:
"A Glimpse of Wisdom Through the Feminine" by Betty DeShong Meador
"Conscious Femininity: Toward a New Cultural Ethos" by Marion Woodman

NEW YORK

Analytical Psychology Society of
  Western New York
166 Cleveland Avenue
Buffalo, NY 14222
(716) 885-1138 or 882-0446

The **Society** grew out of a **Centerpoint** group and was incorporated in 1976. Their library is open to the public, and they sell mail-order both books and tapes. Some examples of tapes:
"Wind and Sun, Fire and Night" by Robert Duncan
"Walking the Dog" by Robert Creeley
"Kundalini: Tibetan Yoga and a Psychology of the

Body" by David L. Miller
Some lectures include:
"Analytical Psychology and the Spiritual Journey" by Wallace and Jean Clift
"Dragon Energy" by Patricia Berry-Hillman and Camille Maurine

C.G. Jung Center
28 East 39th Street
New York, NY 10016
(212) 697-6430

The **C.G. Jung Center** includes the following:
"**The C.G. Jung Foundation for Analytical Psychology, Inc.** was chartered in 1962. Its purposes are to disseminate the work and thought of Carl Gustav Jung and to develop understanding of the range and applicability of analytical psychology. Lectures, seminar series, film showings, symposia, and workshops are open both to members and to the general public." For example:
"Folksong: A Lost World of Archetypes" by Robertson Davies
"Sky Gods and Secret Lovers" by Diana Beach
"Aging: Old Bottles, New Wine" by Adolf Guggenbuhl-Craig
The **C.G. Jung Foundation Book Service** has a wide selection of books on and related to analytical psychology. They are available by mail or by direct sale. See #7. Call (212) 697-6433.
The **C.G. Jung Institute of New York** offers a six-year training program for qualified persons wishing to become Jungian analysts. See #10. Call (212) 986-5458.
The **C.G. Jung Therapy Center** is a low-cost therapy center. Call (212) 986-5458.
ARAS (The Archive for Research in Archetypal Symbolism) is a research and study center located at the **C.G. Jung Center**. See #8. Call (212) 697-3480.

"The Analytical Psychology Club of New York, Inc. was founded in 1946 to provide an opportunity for those who have had Jungian analysis to meet for the exchange of ideas, thoughts, and feelings about analytical psychology. Membership is open to applicants who have completed the required number of hours of Jungian analysis and who have been recommended by a qualified analyst. Some lectures sponsored by the **Club** are open to **Foundation** members as well as to the general public."

The **Kristine Mann Library** is an outstanding collection of works on and related to analytical psychology. See #8. Call (212) 697-7877.

Quadrant is a semi-annual journal published by the **Center.** See #5.

Dialogue House
80 E. 11th Street
New York, NY 10003
(212) 673-5880 or (800) 221-5844

"Dialogue House, since its inception in 1966, has been committed to the belief that a modern democracy can make it possible for each member of the community to experience the principle of creativity in his or her own life. Toward this goal **Dialogue House** has been engaged in extensive social/personal programs":

The **National Intensive Journal Program** makes about 500 authorized **Intensive Journal** workshops a year available in the United States, Canada, England, etc. They include:

The Life Context Workshop
The Depth Contact Workshop
The Life Integration Workshop
Dialogue House also publishes books. For example:
The Dynamics of Hope by Ira Progoff
Jung's Psychology and its Social Meaning by Ira Progoff.

Jungian Society of Rochester
c/o Liz and Herb Greenberg
10 Harrison Circle
Pittsford, NY 14534
(716) 248-3235

Recent lectures:
"Fairy Tale Interpretation" by Catherine Johnson
"Moses: An Archetype of the Patriarch and the Abandoned Child" by Herbert Greenberg

Wainwright House
Center for Development of Human Potential
260 Stuyvesant Avenue
Rye, NY 10580
(914) 967-6080

"**Wainwright House** is a non-profit, non-sectarian educational organization dedicated to the development of the human potential in a changing world. In addition to its **Institute for the Study of Depth Psychology, Wainwright House** provides seminars, conferences and on-going programs in the arts, business, global issues, health and religion.

Wainwright House has long been a center for the study of the disciplines related to depth psychology, with emphasis on Jungian studies. By adding new courses with specific clinical emphasis, the **Institute** expects to expand its public audience and to meet the needs of mental health professionals in the Westchester-Fairfield area."

Among its recent offerings:
"Psyche and Symbol: An Introduction to Jung's Psychology" by Franklin E. Vilas, Jr.
"Subtle Body, Dense Mind: A Seminar on Bodywork and Psychotherapy" by Roger Woolger
"C.S. Lewis: The Visionary Christian" by Brewster Beach

C.G. Jung Society of Central New York
P.O. Box 6706
Syracuse, NY 13217
(315) 474-6094

"The **C.G. Jung Society of Central New York** is a non-profit, educational organization which aims to disseminate and explore the ideas of C.G. Jung, as well as related material from mythology, dance and movement, literature, art and religion. We do this primarily through our member organized lectures and workshops, as listed in our thrice-yearly program brochures. We sponsor nationally known lecturers on Jungian topics, and also programs by local presenters."
    Lectures given:
    What Is Reality?" by Paul Kugler
    "The Archetype as River" by Steve Simmer

NORTH CAROLINA

C.G. Jung Society of the Triangle Area
510 Caswell Road
Chapel Hill, NC 27514
(919) 929-2607

"Our **Society** exists to share the teaching of C.G. Jung, and it was founded on January 14, 1983. Membership is by annual dues, with the **Society** open to anyone interested in Jung's psychology. We offer a monthly newsletter to members."
    Recent lectures:
    "C.G. Jung and Mysticism" by John Yungblut
    "Dreams: The Hidden Doors of the Psyche" by Marjorie Skott

Charlotte Friends of Jung
c/o Allen Boyer
1232 Townes

Charlotte, NC 28209
(704) 527-7457

The Unicorn Hunter
1415 Biltmore Drive
Charlotte, NC 28207
(704) 334-4095

The **Unicorn Hunter** "sponsors workshops on journal writing and dream work, and networks information about silent retreats, meditation and programs organized by **Charlotte Friends of Jung.**"

Kanuga
An Episcopal Center
P.O. Drawer 250
Hendersonville, NC 28793
(704) 692-9136

"**Kanuga** was established as an arm of the Episcopal Church in 1928. Our primary mission is to provide an environment, formal and informal programs, and facilities for an experience in Christian community which will help people reaffirm the power of Christ and exercise their responsibility for growth in Christian community, wherever they may be.

We frequently host groups who conduct conferences, meetings, and training schools for a variety of education and scientific purposes. When we are serving as a logistical support platform for other people's programs our primary objective is to provide a setting for personal growth.

Kanuga hosts the annual fall "Journey Into Wholeness" conference (see #4) and presents "The Way of the Dream" film series each spring.

We publish a quarterly **Kanuga News,** have a small private library which contains the **Collected Works of C.G. Jung,** and operate a bookstore."

Community for Individuation
P.O. Box 786
Huntersville, NC 28078
(704) 875-1514

OHIO

Jung Association of Greater Cincinnati
7945 Graves Road
Cincinnati, OH 45243

A recent lecture:
"The Archetypal Reality of Everyday Life as Expressed in Literature, Art and Experience" by Anthony Stevens

Jung Educational Center of Cleveland
c/o Vocata George
33 E. 5th Avenue
Berea, OH 44017
(216) 243-6875

"Vocata George founded the **Center** to provide education and therapy according to the concepts of Jungian psychology in the Cleveland area. Classes are taught in "Introduction to C.G. Jung", "Dream Work", and "Goddess Exploration".

C.G. Jung Association of Miami Valley
734 Harmon Avenue
Dayton, OH 45419
(513) 293-4856

A recent lecture:
"The Archetypes of War and Peace" by Anthony Stevens

OREGON

Tools for Inner Growth
Box 520
Chiloquin, OR 97624

That's us, folks. Perched on a hill in the middle of a national forest, we are one of the smallest of the new small presses. (See the back pages for ordering information.)

In addition to books, we offer the following workshops:

"A Practical Introduction to Psychological Types" (see #3)

"Jung and the Life of Prayer". Is Jung's psychology compatible with Christian faith? Can it really help in the life of prayer? This workshop is directed to those who have a serious interest in the life of prayer and would like to explore their hopes and misgivings about the use of Jung's psychology in it. It deals with Jung's attitude toward Christianity and the concrete interactions that can take place between psychological development and spiritual growth.

Oregon Friends of C.G. Jung
185 Pine Valley Road
Lake Oswego, OR 97034
(503) 635-3904

"The Oregon Friends of C.G. Jung was organized in the fall of 1974 with the purpose of furthering the knowledge of and interest in the psychology of Carl Jung.

Statewide membership is drawn from a variety of backgrounds and professions and is open to anyone sincerely interested in the work of Carl Jung.

Dues are modest and members are given special courtesies in admissions to programs and in registrations for workshops. Membership privileges also include the borrowing of books and cassette tapes from our ever-growing library.

Oregon Friends of Jung also sponsors **Centerpoint** - an opportunity to study Jungian psychology in a small group of 6-8 participants.

Recent lectures:

"The Healing Edge of Madness in the Borderline Personality" by Nathan Schwartz-Salant

"The Passive Aggressive Male" by David Hart

"Oedipus" by Peter Montgomery

PENNSYLVANIA

Kirkridge
Bangor, PA 18013
(215) 588-1793

"**Kirkridge** is a center rooted in Christ where people on pilgrimage seek community in the midst of diversity and experience the transforming power of the Spirit for personal wholeness, reconciliation, justice in the world.

Since 1942 Kirkridge retreat and study center has welcomed pilgrims seeking solitude and community, rest and discernment, towards personal and social transformation.

Kirkridge is located on one hundred cares of mountainside in northeastern Pennsylvania. The Appalachian Trail runs through our property at the top of the mountain, where vistas are long. In the valley, gentle pastureland surrounds our 1815 farmhouse. You will find the facilities modest but comfortable, the meals simple but pleasing. In this setting, simplicity and conservation of resources will seem like natural responses to the earth's own gifts of healing and grounding."

Recent Jungian-oriented weekends:

"In the Wilderness: The Spiritual Dimensions of Depression" by Brewster Beach

"Training in the Art of Healing and Spiritual Guidance" by Morton Kelsey

C.G. Jung Center of Philadelphia
2008 Chancellor Street
Philadelphia, PA 19103
(215) 557-7545

The **C.G. Jung Center of Philadelphia** has a library and program of lectures. Recent topics:
"The Problem of Evil" by Uwe Steffen
"The Comedy of Life" by James Hollis
"Enfeeblement" by Alexander McCurdy

The C.G. Jung Educational Center of Pittsburgh
4527 Winthrop Street
Pittsburgh, PA 15213
(412) 681-1235 or 366-3024

The **C.G. Jung Educational Center of Pittsburgh** organizes seminars, lectures, workshops, and study groups on the subject of the Analytical Psychology of C.G. Jung.

The educational programs sponsored by the **Center** are led by visiting and local experts on Jungian psychology and open to professional and lay individuals alike." It was founded in 1975.

"Members of the **Center** come from a variety of fields - psychology, education, business, health, law, the arts, and religion - and include both practitioners and lay people."

They have a library of books and tapes, and they publish the **Phoenix,** their newsletter.

Past activities include:

Courses: "Introduction to Analytical Psychology" and "Dreams and Healing"

"Marriage and/or Individuation" by Murray Stein

"Depression and Analytical Psychology" by Judith Hubbock

Workshops: "Fairy Tales" by James Hillman and "Our Many Selves in Marriage" by Jan and Murray Stein

Pittsburgh Jung Society
5654 Darlington Road
Pittsburgh, PA 15217
(412) 682-8172

"**The Pittsburgh Jung Society** aims to meet some of the educational and professional needs of the Pittsburgh Community and the tri-state area by offering lectures and seminars on the ideas of C.G. Jung and contemporary thought in the area of Analytical Psychology. It evolved out of the **Pittsburgh Jung Seminar.** We have no membership requirements at this time."
A recent lecture:
"Beyond the Feminine Principle: A Post-Jungian Viewpoint" by Andrew Samuels

The Jung Society of Scranton
c/o Eugene Monick
Waverly Road, Glenburn
Dalton, PA 18414
(717) 563-1251

Jesuit Center for Spiritual Growth
Typrofile Press
Box 223, Church Road
Wernersville, PA 19565
(215) 678-3886

The **Jesuit Center for Spiritual Growth** runs a wide variety of different kinds of retreats, workshops and training programs, some of which are Jungian-oriented. For example:
"Adult Growth, Development and Eastering" by George Schemel, which concentrates on mid-life tran-

sitions from a Jungian point of view and which makes use of the Myers-Briggs Type Indicator
  "Dreams" by Jack Mostyn
  Typrofile Press produces the booklet "Facing Your Type", which explains psychological types in connection with the MBTI.

TENNESSEE

C.G. Jung Society of Knoxville
Fountain City Presbyterian Church
500 Hotel Road
Knoxville, TN 37918
(615) 688-2163

"The **C.G. Jung Society of Knoxville** was founded by Jack Davis in 1984. The purpose of the **Society** is to give all interested persons an opportunity to discuss and become better acquainted with the thought of C.G. Jung and to experience the positive growth possible through an openness to the Unconscious. Persons of all or no religious persuasion are especially invited to explore the religious dimensions of the thought of Jung.
  The **Society** sponsors a weekly Tuesday evening discussion. In addition, there are retreats, Journal Workshops, the presentation of guest lecturers, art therapy and opportunities for individual therapy."

Dorothea M. Mills
9221 Topoco Road
Knoxville, TN 37922-3674
(615) 261-4403

  Questpoint, Centerpoint and Therapy groups are on-going.

TEXAS

Jung Society of Austin
4000 Avenue B
Austin, TX 78751
(512) 453-3635

"The **Jung Society of Austin** is a society of lay-people interested in studying the philosophy and psychology of Carl Jung. Our **Society** is here because Ethel Nisley decided to open a Jungian bookstore in Austin. She met me at a seminar at the **Jung Institute** in Houston where she was a volunteer librarian for eleven years. I (Yolande Moeller) agreed to start the **Society** and it has been a very warm and symbiotic arrangement. Our classes and our reception area are in the bookstore, though separate, and we are a separate non-profit organization."

The **Society** offers classes, lectures and workshops:

"Creating a Visual Journal" by Jan Mikkelsen
"The Dark Side of Marriage" by Arthur Travis
"Chemistry That Matters" by Michael Bauza

The **Society** also publishes **Jung Society of Austin,** a monthly newsletter.

The Analytical Psychology Association of Dallas
10118 Medlock Drive
Dallas, TX 75218
(214) 348-7284 or 369-2350

The **Analytical Psychology Association of Dallas** sponsors lectures, seminars and classes. For example:

"The Archetypal Self" by James Hall
"Conscious Femininity" by Marion Woodman
"The Dream World" by Ronald Schenk

The **Association** also publishes a newsletter.

The Dallas Institute of Humanities and Culture
2719 Routh Street
Dallas, TX 75201
(214) 698-9090

"**The Dallas Institute** exists to care for the actual things of the urban world. In some instances, these things are visible - the city, education, architecture, medicine, art, technology, money. Equally important are the invisible forms within which life takes place and has meaning - friendship, the soul, taste, imagination, community, intellectual life, ritual, leadership.
Some publications include:
Water & Dreams: An Essay on the Imagination of Matter by Gaston Bachelard
Images of the Untouched by Joanne Stroud & Gail Thomas, eds.
The lecture series includes:
"The Cultural Psychology of Rudolf Steiner, Medicine and Nutrition" by Robert Sardello
"Kore: Divine Maiden" by Eileen Gregory
The Dallas Institute Forum "is a unique gathering of people willing to express ideas in the liberty of a classic forum - a receptive audience of open minds. **The Forum** meets once a month for discussion luncheons from January to May." The 1987 theme is "Design for Community."

C.G. Jung Institute of Dallas
P.O. Box 7004
Dallas, TX 75209-0004
(214) 353-2911

"The aims of the **Institute** are for the eventual training of Jungian Analysts and the concomitant professional society that this would create. The **Institute** originated with three analysts in 1980, who incorporated at that time. Since then three more analysts have moved to Dallas, and the **Institute** has begun to organize.

Our future plans include the eventual training of Jungian Analysts in the Metroplex. While the actual training of analysts is still in the planning stage, you may wish to participate in our professional meetings as a member of your own discipline. We have several categories of membership, therefore one does not have to be a Certified Jungian Analyst to belong."

C.G. Jung Educational Center of Houston, Texas, Inc.
5200 Montrose Boulevard
Houston, TX 77006-6597
(713) 524-8253

"The **Jung Center** is a place for personal growth, reflection, integration, healing and renewal in a supportive, peaceful atmosphere.

Located near The Museum of Fine Arts and across the street from the Cullen Sculpture Garden, the **Center** is the oldest of its kind in the world. It was chartered by the State of Texas in 1958. Dr. Jung gave formal permission to use his name in the **Center's** title and remained a strong supporter of its programs until his death in 1961. The **Jung Center** is unique in offering an ongoing program in the Expressive Arts (body movement, painting, clay sand tray) as a way of integrating Dr. Jung's psychological concepts", and a series of open lectures and seminars for the public. In addition to the educational programs, analytical and counseling referral services are available.

Recent examples:

Lecture: "Growth and Growing Older" by Martha Shelton-Wolf

Course: "The Psychology of Cinderella" by Nina Tucci

Seminar: "Transitions in Step-Parenthood" by Carol Brady and Stephen Pollack

"The **Center's** Ethel Carradine Kurth Library and

Bookstore have an extensive selection of books in the fields of psychology, religion and the expressive arts. It also maintains a mail order service for the purchase of books.

In addition to all of these services, the **Center** sponsors art exhibits in complimentary to Jungian philosophy throughout the year that are open to the public without charge."

UTAH

Provo Friends of Jung
1060 East 800 South
Drem, UT 84058
(801) 225-5203

Lectures, seminars and group meetings are scheduled.

C.G. Jung Study Group
4521 South 480 East
Salt Lake City, UT 84107
(801) 266-6908

The **C.G. Jung Study Group** started in the 1960s and they meet each Tuesday.

1st and 3rd Tuesdays: "The Basics of Jungian Psychology"

2nd and 4th Tuesdays: "Advanced Jungian Studies"

VIRGINIA

Studies in Jungian Thought
The Department of Philosophy and
The Institute of Humanities
Old Dominion University
Norfolk, VA 23508
(804) 440-3861

"In conjunction with the aims and activities of the Institute of Humanities of Old Dominion University, the Department of Philosophy offers a unique program of graduate courses titled **Studies in Jungian Thought.** Utilizing Jung's **Collected Works** these courses seek to provide graduate students with a basic theoretical foundation for understanding Jung's complex system of ideas." The courses are:
"Structures of the Psyche"
"Phenomenology of the Self"
"Individuation"
"Creativity and the Work of Art"
They also sponsor the Jungian Retreat in the Swiss Alps called "Images of Transformation". See #4.

C.G. Jung Society of Tidewater
Norfolk, VA
(804) 481-3902

Virginia Wesleyan College
Wesleyan Drive
Norfolk, VA 23502

They have seminars on "C.G. Jung and The Symbolic Life".

Jungian Venture
8125 Whittington Drive
Richmond, VA 23235
(804) 272-0923

A recent offering:
"God and the Gods" by Philip Zabriskie

WASHINGTON

Bellingham Friends of Jung
4200 Meridian, Suite 202

Bellingham, WA 98225
(206) 733-6388
and
3126 West Broadway
Vancouver, BC
Canada V6K 2H2

The **Bellingham Friends of Jung** offer Jungian and Process Workshops. Recent topics:
"On the Dreaming Body" by David Roomy
"Winter Depression and Other Hoary Ghosts"

Pacific Northwest Society of Jungian Analysts
c/o William Willeford
905 Federal Avenue East
Seattle, WA 98102
(206) 323-6344

"The **Pacific Northwest Society of Jungian Analysts** was founded in 1983. The purposes of the organization are:
to facilitate educational and research activities related to analytical psychology
to establish basic requirements and to encourage the maintenance of high standards of excellence for training and practice of Jungian analysis
to encourage an accurate understanding in the study of concepts of analytical psychology
Our members reside in Oregon, Washington and British Columbia."

C.G. Jung Society
P.O. Box 31067
Seattle, WA 98103
(206) 525-3287

"Established in Seattle in 1972, the group seeks to promote an understanding of Jung's analytical psychology and the current use of Jungian concepts by contemporary thinkers. One of many such groups throughout the world, the **C.G. Jung Society** sponsors monthly lectures and seminars by local and nationally known Jungian scholars. We also maintain a reference library and coordinate Centerpoint and book discussion groups. Membership is open to anyone interested in learning about Jungian thought. Membership privileges include free or reduced admission to monthly lectures, registration priority and reduced rates on seminars, and use of the library."

Recent offerings include:

"The Blues" by William Willeford

"Psychological Types" by William H. Levy

WISCONSIN

Hancock Center for Movement Arts & Therapies, Inc.
16 North Hancock Street
Madison, WI 53703
(608) 251-0908

"**Hancock Center for Movement Arts & Therapies, Inc.** is a nonprofit organization created to promote the informed and effective use of dance/movement therapy in the Midwest. It offers workshops, classes and resources for the professional and general public. Groups and individual dance/movement therapy sessions and Alexander technique classes are given on a regular basis. It has two dance studios, conference rooms, a reference library, and audio-visual equipment."

A recent weekend symposium:

"Psycholanalytic Approaches to Dance/Movement Therapy" by Penny L. Bernstein, Liljan Espenak and Elaine V. Siegel

CANADA

ALBERTA

Tad and Noreen Guzie
5267 Dalcroft Crescent N.W.
Calgary, Alberta T3A IN6
(403) 286-0209

"Tad and Noreen give workshops for adults throughout the United States and Canada. Their workshops focus on psychological types and archetypes, communication skills, and decision-making processes.

Examples of workshops:

"About Men and Women: Finding Identity and Fulfillment" "Why do some men and women appear aggressive, while others seem to be more caring? Why do some male types get along better with some female types? And what happens when a person, suddenly, in the middle of life, feels moved to live out a different story?"

"Understanding Your Psychological Type: The Myers-Briggs Type Indicator" "This workshop offers a thorough explanation of Jung's theory of type, with the help of the Myers-Briggs Type Indicator."

Friends of Jung
c/o Evangeline Kane
7829-111 Avenue
Edmonton, Alberta T5H 1L1
429-4314

Recent activities include a series of six talks entitled, "Fall Down and Kiss the Earth: Recovering Soul Consciousness"

BRITISH COLUMBIA

The C.G. Jung Society of Vancouver
c/o Lynette Walker
23541 24th Avenue
Langley, B.C. V3A 789
(604) 534-8247

Recent offerings:
"Varieties of Transference" by Bonnelle Strickling
"Speak Up Say Be Quiet", a performance with Moira Molholland

NEW BRUNSWICK

East Coast Group
c/o Keltie Campbell
11 Orchard Drive
Moncton, N.B. E1E 3K9

Centre for Psycho Alchemy
c/o Paul McCracken
333 Beverley Crescent
Riverview, N.B. E03 385

ONTARIO

The C.G. Jung Society of Ottawa
15 Lakeside Avenue
Ottawa, Ont. K1S 3H1
(613) 731-3132 or 235-9411

"The C.G. Jung Society of Ottawa was founded to provide opportunities for people to further their understanding of the work of Carl Gustav Jung, including its application to their own self-development. The Society, founded in May 1979, organizes lectures, workshops, and informal discussions, and operates a library and bookselling facility.

Workshops or lectures are held approximately twice per month, from September to Jung. An annual meeting is held in the spring."

Recent programs include:

"Hags and Heroes: A Jungian/Feminist Approach to Psychotherapy with Couples" by Polly Young-Eisendrath and Ed Epstein

"Jung and the Problem of God" by James Forsyth

C.G. Jung Foundation of the Analytical Society of Ontario

223 St. Clair Avenue, West
Toronto, Ont. M4V 1R3
(416) 961-9767

"As the **Foundation's** interests include all aspects of mental experience within its structure, special interest groups meet to discuss psychological experience from different viewpoints. For example, there is a Journal Discussion Group of working professionals in the fields of psychiatry, psychology, social work and psychiatric care, a Pastoral Psychology Group founded by clergy but open to all interested parties. Similarly, there is an Educator's Group which though founded by teachers is also open to all those interested in education."

Recent offerings:

"Symbols of Transformation: Alchemy and Individuation" by Nathan Schwartz-Salant

"The Power of the Ring" by Dieter Baumann

QUEBEC

C.G. Jung Society of Montreal

4361 Wilson Avenue
Montreal, Que. H4A 2V3

"The C.G. Jung Society of Montreal was founded in April 1975 by a small number of individuals who felt their interest in Analytical Psychology could best be served by a pooling of information and resources, and the promotion of an ongoing programme of lectures, workshops and study groups.

The membership is diverse, with individuals drawn from a variety of cultural, educational and occupational backgrounds. As the programmes and resources are in English, active participation in the life of the **Society** requires a working knowledge of that language.

The aim of the **Society** is to provide opportunities for the experience of Jungian psychology, whether it be through the one to one relationship of individual analysis, or group interaction of workshops and study and interest groups.

We have a newsletter, a modest book service, and a small library."

Recent programs:

"What Are Archetypes?" by David L. Miller, Ginette Paris and Naomi Golderberg

"Opening Channels to the Creative" by Edith Wallace

Le Cercle C.G. Jung de Montreal
B.P. 457
Succ. Youville
Montreal, QC H2P 2V6
(514) 288-1080

2 LOCAL AND PROFESSIONAL GROUPS AROUND THE WORLD

AUSTRALIA

The C.G. Jung Society of Sydney, New South Wales
G.P.O. Box 2796
Syndey, 2001
747.2707

"**The C.G. Jung Society of Sydney, New South Wales,** was founded in 1975. The **Society** aims to awaken among people a greater awareness of the influence and workings of the unconscious in their lives and to explore ways of working with the unconscious. Its meetings aim to provide a forum where questions about the inner psychological journey are discussed.

Membership is open to any member of the public, and lecture topics are announced in the Saturday Morning Herald on the day of the lecture.

The Library consists of a fine up-to-date selection of Jungian and Jungian-related books and tapes."

They publish a newsletter as well.

Recent events:
"Working with One's Dreams and the Unconscious" by Janice Daw
"Anxiety and Guilt" by Mario Jacoby
"On Being a Man" by Joel Ryce-Menuhin

Australian and New Zealand Society of Jungian Analysts
c/o Alison Anne Noonan
55 Mandalong Road
Mosman, N.S.W. 2088
02-960 1698

"The small training group meets a full day each month, and since we are in the beginning stages of building up resources, we would be glad to hear from any group which has books, tapes, films, Journals, etc., which they no longer need: these would be greatly valued!"

AUSTRIA

Österreichische Gesellschaft für Analytische Psychologie
c/o Mag.Dr. Reinhard Skolek
Hochmaisgasse 4/1/3
1130 Wien, Austria
(0222) 63.57.11

The **Society** was founded in 1980 by Austrian Jungians. The goals are:
    depth psychology research
    education in the area of Jungian psychology
    psychotherapy
They have a library which is open only to group members.

BELGIUM

Société Belge de Psychologie Analytique
Belgische Vereniging voor Analytische Psychologie
Avenue J.B. Depaire 91
1020 Bruxelles, Belgium
02/479.78.49

"Our **Society** was founded in 1975 in order to advance the study of analytical psychology, to encourage and to maintain a high level of training and practice, to provide a training program, and to organize national and international exchanges, especially with the **International Association for Analytical Psychology.**"

BRAZIL

Sociedade Brasileira de Psicologia Analítica
Rua Livramento, 133
4008 Sao Paulo
884 4180
and
R. Almirante Pereira Guimaraes 72 -CJ.504/505
02240 Rio de Janeiro
239 2246

The **Sociedade Brasileira de Psicologia Analítica** was founded in Sao Paulo on March 13, 1978. The objective of the **Sociedade** is to disseminate analytical psychology through courses, conferences and publications. Since 1979 the **Sociedade** has maintained the course for the formation of analysts with the purpose of training candidates within the Jungian concepts. Beginning this year our library is open to the general public. The **Sociedade** publishes the **Junguiana.** See #5.

Some courses and conferences are open to the public. Past examples:

"The Masculine and Feminine in the Development of the Personality" by Malvina E. Muszkat

"Woman: the creative conflict between being a mother and a professional" by Iraci Galias

DENMARK

Jung-Institutet
Gl. Kongevej 47 B
DK 1610 Kobenhavn V

This Jungian group in Copenhagen offers lectures and seminars in Danish and also occasionally in English. A program is sent out twice a year.

ENGLAND

Association of Jungian Analysts
Flat 3, 7 Eton Avenue
London NW3 3EL
01-794 8711

"**The Association of Jungian Analysts** offers a training programme in Analytical Psychology and on the approach to Analytical Psychotherapy which has grown from Jung's model of the psyche. The training course is concerned with clinical, personal, intellectual and spiritual aspects of individual development."
Training includes seminars, personal analysis and supervised control analyses.
They have a library which is not open to the public.
Past lectures:
"The Wise Old Man and the Messy Baby" by Mara Sidoli
"Astrology and Analysis" by Liz Greene

Society of Analytical Psychology and the
    C.G. Jung Clinics
1, Daleham Gardens
London, NW3 5BY
01-435 7696

"The declared aims of the **Society of Analytical Psychology** are to promote and encourage the practice and application of analytical psychology. It provides education and training for candidates to become analysts and opportunities for the understanding and use of analytical psychology for psychotherapists in various fields.
At the **Society's** foundation in 1946 there were seven members, most of whom had known and worked with Jung. It has grown steadily since then and there are now (1986) over 120 members as well as an in-

creasing number of trainees. Analytical psychologists work in three settings: (1) in private practice; (2) for the **C.G. Jung Clinic** to offer analysis to patients with limited means and (3) in psychiatric hospitals and departments of general hospitals, in child guidance clinics, universities and a variety of voluntary agencies.

The **C.G. Jung Clinics** for adult and for child patients each provide analysis for those who could not otherwise afford it.

An intensive training in the analysis of adults is offered to candidates who are suitably qualified in medicine or other appropriate disciplines such as psychology, social work and pastoral care. The prospective candidates' own analysis is the most crucial part of their training. This ensures that they gain insight into personal conflicts and learn from the experience of being a patient.

The training for child analysis, founded in 1973, includes the supervised analysis of children of various ages including adolescents as well as a parent."

They publish **The Journal of Analytical Psychology** (see #5), as well as a series of books called **The Library of Analytical Psychology.** (see #6)

"We do have a library which is for the exclusive use of our own students and members."

The British Association of Psychotherapists
121, Hendon Lane
London N3 3PR
01-346 1747

The **British Association of Psychotherapists** is a training organization. They have a library, but it is not open to the public. They publish an annual which may include some of the lectures given during the year.

Analytical Psychology Club
37 York Street Chambers
York Street
London W1H 1DE

The **Analytical Psychology Club** publishes **Harvest.**
(see #5) It also sponsors lectures.

The Independent Group of Analytical Psychologists
P.O. Box 396
London N1 2JD

Guild of Pastoral Psychology
37 Hogarth Hill
London, NW11 6AY
01-458-3125

"The **Guild of Pastoral Psychology** offers a meeting ground for all those interested in the relationship between religion and depth psychology, particularly the work of C.G. Jung and his followers. Depth psychology has contributed many new insights into the meaning of religion and its symbols and their relevance to everyday life. The **Guild** provides a means of communicating the results of recent practice and research to everyone interested professionally or personally."

The **Guild** is celebrating its Golden Jubilee. (1937-1987) The **Guild** has many affiliated groups and a library.

Recent lectures and conferences:

"Alchemy in Modern Perspective" by B.D. Goodwin

"Spiritual Direction and Counselling - Is There a Difference?" by Gerard Hughes

"The Child" by Joel Ryce-Menuhin

The **Guild** lectures are available in pamphlet form. See #6.

FRANCE

Société Française de Psychologie Analytique
1 Place de l'Ecole Militaire
75005 Paris
45.55.42.90

The **Société** is a French training group that was founded in 1969.
Past lectures and workshops:
"Incest and Sacrifice" by Pierre Solie
"Alchemy and Mythology" by Gilbert Masse
"The Playing Space" by Genevieve Guy-Gillet

Groupe d'Etudes C.G. Jung
1 Place de l'Ecole Militaire
75005 Paris
45.55.42.90

The **Groupe d'Etudes C.G. Jung** was formed to make known the thought and work of C.G. Jung. It was founded in 1926 by Jean Bruneton, and is one of the oldest in the world. Jung, himself, came in 1932 to give a conference on the collective unconscious.
Recent programs:
"La Synchronicite, d'après mon expérience" by Monique Leterrier
"Adam et Eve: un mythe Fondateur de l'individuation" by Marie-Laure Colonna
"Quelle Societe Demain? Alienation Religieuse ou Individuation?" by Darius Shayegan
They publish **Cahiers Jungiens de Psychanalyse** (see #5) as well as a library and a book store. In addition they have an extensive collection of tapes of past lectures for sale.

GERMANY

Deutsche Gesellschaft fuer Analytische Psychologie
1000 Berlin 37
Schützallee 118
(030) 831.20.96

ISRAEL

Israel Association of Analytical Psychology
c/o H. Yehezkel Kluger
Hatzofim Street 4
Mt. Carmel, 34352 Haifa
(04) 38.62.94

ITALY

Associazione Italiana per lo Studio della
    Psicologia Analitica
Via Cola di Rienzo 28
00192 Roma
38.82.10

Centro Italiano de Psicologia Analitica
Via Po, 42
00198 Roma
(06) 86.36.36
    and
Piazzale Libia 5
20135 Milano
(02) 57.38.17

Teatro di Marionette del Ramerino
Via dello Stracchino, 25
50065 Pontassieve, Firenze
(055) 830.45.33

The marionette group formed around Silvana
Radogna in 1973, and consists of people interested

in the world of the psyche, and discovering the inner meaning of theater. They have created three plays:
"Harlequin Corpse and Doctor Against His Will"
"The Two Bewitched Sisters"
"The Moon, the Devil and the Seven Sisters"
"They are a means for the surfacing of the psychic, the spiritual, the soul, if they help us to leave out the egoic, the literal imitation of reality, the obvious, and through their fantastic role they lend themselves to being a fertile earthly restorer for our imaginal."

SWITZERLAND

C.G. Jung Institut Zürich
Hornweg 28
8700 Küsnacht
01/910 53 23

"The C.G. Jung Institute of Zürich was established in 1948 as a private, non-profit foundation for training and research in analytical psychology. At the request of its founders, Dr. Jung himself drew up the original plans for the Institute and served as the first president of its governing board. He continued to guide its teaching and research activities until his death in 1961.
In addition to the training of Jungian analysts, which is its principal activity, it promotes the further development of the concepts and methods of analytical psychology in a variety of ways - by making its facilities available to researchers, sponsoring publication of works by Jungian authors, and providing the setting for an on-going exchange between practicing analysts, scholars, and scientists."
The activities of the Institute include:
the training program (see #10)
a special training program in child and adolescent psychotherapy

the **Counseling Center,** which "serves approximately 500 people per year, and advanced trainees conduct over 20,000 hours of analysis and psychotherapy
with patients of limited financial means at fees
about 25% of normal rates."
bookstore (no mail ordering)
library (see #8)
an extensive program in continuing education.
Many of the courses in the training program are open
to auditors with around 400 auditors regularly attending one or more course per semester.
There is both a German and English program.
Recent English lectures, seminars and colloquia:
"The Missing Father" by I. Baker
"Two Icons and their Spiritual Meaning" by H.
Hoerni-Jung
"Empathy" by F. Bleibler
"Pictorial Self-Representation" by R. Isaac

**Association of Graduate Analytical Psychologists
of the C.G. Jung Institute Zürich**
C.G. Jung Institute
Hornweg 28
8700 Küsnacht/Zürich
01-910.53.23

**Schweizerische Gesellschaft Fuer Analytische
Psychologie**
Postfach 115
8042 Zürich

International Association for Analytical Psychology
Postfach 115
8042 Zürich

The **International Association** is comprised of all
Jungian professional groups. It publishes a list of
members (see #10) and holds an international conference. (see #4)

3 PSYCHOLOGICAL TYPES

APT (The Association for Psychological Types)
CAPT (Center for Applications of Psychological Type)
2720 N.W. 6th Street
Gainesville, FL 32609
(904) 375-0160

APT and CAPT are two independent but coordinated organizations devoted to the development and diffusion of knowledge about psychological types through the MBTI.

"The Myers-Briggs Type Indicator (MBTI) is a questionnaire developed by Isabel Briggs Myers and her mother, Katharine C. Briggs, to facilitate use of that part of the theory of C.G. Jung which is concerned with what Jung referred to as psychological types. The essence of the theory is that variations in behavior which may seem random are actually consistent and orderly when one understands differences in the ways people prefer to take in information and make decisions.

In 1969 Isabel Briggs Myers began a collaboration with Mary H. McCaulley who was a clinical psychologist at the University of Florida. To further their joint research, a Typology Laboratory was set up at the University. By 1975 the Laboratory outgrew its academic setting and the Center for Applications of Psychological Type was established."

CAPT (Center for Applications of Psychological Type)

"CAPT is a non-profit organization whose aim is to help foster the understanding and constructive use of differences among people. CAPT provides a variety of services to further understanding of psychological types:

Workshops: CAPT workshops provide training in the theory, research, and practical application of the MBTI."

Recent Workshops:

"Using Type in Ministry"

"Type Differences and the Experience of Loss"

"An Orientation to Type Theory and the Instrument"

"**Consultant Services:** CAPT provides services to organizations and groups to: (1) introduce type theory and practical applications of the MBTI, and (2) provide ongoing consultation.

Publications: CAPT publishes and distributes a large variety of materials about the MBTI - books, research reports, teaching aids, and computer software for MBTI research and cassette tapes. CAPT also distributes MBTI Testing Materials to professionally qualified MBTI users. Publications by CAPT itself include:

Jung's Theory of Psychological Types and the Myers-Briggs Type Indicator by Mary H. McCaulley

The Myers Longitudinal Medical Study: Monograph II by Mary H. McCaulley

Computer Scoring: CAPT provides computer scoring which includes a report for the person answering the MBTI, a report for the counselor, a type distribution of the group, and statistical information for researchers on cards or tape.

Research Consultation: CAPT research services help MBTI users organize, analyze, and interpret their data. CAPT research consultation ranges from brief answers to specific questions to extended data analyses.

Research Services: CAPT maintains a data bank which is generated by the computer scoring of the MBTI. This data bank can be analyzed for type differences in occupations, age, and educational level. For example, type tables have been created for the "Atlas of Type Tables" and the "MBTI Manual". See #8 for the **MBTI** Bibliography.

Isabel Briggs Myers Memorial Library: Housed at **CAPT,** this library has an extensive collection of type data and is growing daily thanks to donations of dissertations, books, and articles."

APT (Association for Psychological Type)

"Organized in 1979, the **Association for Psychological Type (APT)** is the national membership organization for all persons interested in psychological type. **APT** members are professionals from a variety of fields who seek to extend development, research and application of psychological type theory and the **Myers Briggs Type Indicator. APT** serves as a network bringing together both people and ideas through its programs and publications.

The Bulletin of Psychological Type, APT's national newsletter, is published three times a year. It contains articles, reports and book reviews on a variety of applications of psychological type. It also announces national and regional conferences, training workshops, and other regional interest area events. There is a lively correspondence section where readers share news and views.

National Conferences are held biennially and include detailed presentations of new applications and research in specialty areas, as well as training and skills sessions for persons at all levels.

Regional groups conduct similar but smaller and more frequent meetings in each area of the country.

APT's MBTI Training Program is designed to provide the professional with the basic knowledge necessary for the effective and ethical use of the **MBTI.** It is offered to meet the needs of those already technically qualified to purchase the **Indicator** (but who have little or no training in Psychological Theory and its applications), as well as those in professions which do not typically permit the purchase of psychological tests.

Areas covered include: History and Uses of the **MBTI** Jung's Theory of Psychological Types; Basic principle of Testing and Measurement; Psychometrics of the **MBTI**; Scoring the **MBTI** and the meaning of Scores; Ethical uses of the **MBTI**; Applications of the **MBTI** in various fields.

The training consists of 35-40 hours of pre-session home study using the **APT** 'Home Study Notebook' and required books, followed by the four-day training sessions." The training sessions are held all over the U.S. and Canada.

"**Journal of Psychological Type** is edited by Thomas G. Carskadon, Department of Psychology, P.O. Drawer PF, Mississippi State University, MS 39762. As a service to persons who are interested in the theory, measurement, and applications of psychological type, this journal publishes research and discussion papers relating to the **MBTI** and to Jung's theory of psychological types; papers on other typologies are also considered. Back issues are available from both **CAPT** and **Consulting Psychologists Press.**"

Examples of articles from volume 10:

"The Effect of Jungian Type on Burnout"

"Typing or Stereotyping? Unconscious Bias in Applications of Psychological Type Theory"

"Psychological Type and Interpersonal Compatibility: Evidence for a Relationship Between Communication Style Preference and Relationship Satisfaction in College Roommates"

Consulting Psychologists Press
577 College Avenue
Palo Alto, CA 94306
(415) 857-1444

Consulting Psychologists Press publishes the MBTI and the Singer-Loomis Inventory of Personality (see below) and distributes a number of works on psychological types. Some examples are:

People Types and Tiger Stripes by Gordon Lawrence

Please Understand Me by David Keirsey and Marilyn Bates

Jungian Type Survey

The Jungian Type Survey (also called the Gray-Wheelwrights Test) was first formulated in 1944 by Joseph Wheelwright and Horace Gray, and has gone through a number of revisions. The 15th edition consists of 81 questions, all arranged in a forced-choice format where the test-taker must choose between extraversion and introversion, thinking and feeling, and sensation and intuition. The Jungian Type Survey Manual, and question and answer sheets can be obtained from the C.G. Jung Institute of San Francisco.

MBTI
Carla Rollandini
4705 Exeter Street
Annandale, VA 22003
(703) 941-1858

Carla Rollandini applies the MBTI to "more effective marital communication, organizational development and team building in the workplace, academic and career planning for high school youth and up, and spiritual growth, prayer and life stage development for church and faith communities." She offers the MBTI Introductory Workshop to help groups understand type differences.

New Directions
Consultants in Human Resource Development
P.O. Box 3088
Wayland Square
Providence, RI 02906
(401) 941-6791

New Directions offers workshops and seminars for churches and religious organizations, and non-profit and private groups. All their programs focus on human differences:

"Maintaining Sanity in a Crazy World", a 6-hour session "designed to remove the mystery of why people do things so differently from you"

"Who's In Charge Here, Anyway!", a workshop "that will examine various leadership styles, the strengths of each and why power seems to gravitate to some people"

They also offer programs geared to appreciating the role of human differences in the field of education. For example:

"The Game of Games", a theatrical comic presentation which gives a "revealing look at how we communicate with one another and why those communications are frequently misunderstood."

They distribute **A Matter of Preference,** a booklet about the Myers-Briggs Type Indicator, by Dorothy May Emerson.

Singer-Loomis Inventory of Personality
Consulting Psychologists Press
577 College Avenue
Palo Alto, CA 94306
(415) 857-1444

"The **Singer-Loomis Inventory of Personality (SLIP)** is the work of two Jungian analysts, June Singer and Mary Loomis. After ten years of research, this innovative typology inventory has been developed. This experimental edition introduces an approach to typology that, instead of categorizing persons, points the way to ever widening potentials. The **SLIP** combines Jungian theory with recent findings in personality research." "The **SLIP** attempts to measure 8 cognitive modes independently, avoiding the bi-polarity which Jung suggested and which is used in the **Myers-Briggs Type Indicator.**"

Tools for Inner Growth
Box 520
Chiloquin, OR 97624

"**A Practical Introduction to Psychological Types**" is a workshop that deals with the basic building blocks of typology, type recognition and ways in which type can be developed. It stresses the practical tolerance of differences and how type can be used in community, marriage and family, school situations, etc. It connects Jung's psychological types with William Sheldon's body types.

"**Understanding Your Psychological Type: The Myers-Briggs Type Indicator**"

This is a workshop given by Tad and Noreen Guzie. See p. 57 of the **Guide.**

The Type Reporter
A Quarterly Publication on Psychological Type
524 North Paxton Street
Alexandria, VA 22304
(703) 823-3730

"Each issue of **The Type Reporter** focuses on a theme, such as Careers, Personal Development, Managing, Parenting, Education, Marriage, etc. We interview professionals in that field, talk to people about their personal experiences, and point out the useful texts. Themes allow for more depth in coverage and let you see all the types (including your own), in all sorts of situations.

There are many "theoretical innovators" attracted to this field and **The Type Reporter** is eager to bring you their ideas. For example, in past issues we've presented Scott Golden connecting the language of careers to the language of preferences, Gordon Lawrence speculating on the major dilemmas of each type, and Otto Kroeger's scheme for losing weight according to your type. In our most popular column, called "Every Day," readers contribute advice, humorous anecdotes, and informal hypotheses."

Some article examples for their Vol. 2, No. 1 issue with the theme of "Parents and Children":

"What Made You Such a Special Child?" by Susan Scanlon

""Type Watching": A Favorite Pastime for Parents" by Bob Snipes

"One Family - Four Temperaments" by Lorna A. Barry

4 CONFERENCES

APT Biennial International Conference
APT (The Association for Psychological Type)
2720 N.W. 6th Street
Gainesville, FL 32609
(904) 375-0160

APT (see p. 73) sponsors a biennial conference. The theme of the 1985 conference was "Exploring Our Differences". Some topics were:
"Individuation Through Enlightened Self-Direction" by Kathryn Atman
"Type as an Evolving Psychic Energy System" by Terence Duniho
"Making Decisions Across Psychological Distance" by James Rogers and Edythe Rash Peters
Audiocassette tapes of the conference can be purchased through InfoMedix, 12800 Garden Grove Blvd., Suite F, Garden Grove, CA 92643.

California Spring Conference
c/o C.G. Jung Institute
10349 West Pico Boulevard
Los Angeles, CA 90064
(213) 556-1193

The **California Spring Conference** is held annually for California Jungian analysts and control candidates. It is held in Palm Desert, CA. "The annual spring conference of the three California societies was hosted by the Los Angeles Institute in March 1986." "During the three days together papers on a variety of subjects dealing with Analytical Psychology were presented by Albert Kreinheder, Sigrid McPherson, William Walcott, Mel Ketner, Mary Jo Spencer, and Lawrence Jaffe. There was Greek folk dancing, led by Pan Coukoulis, and poetry shared."

The proceeds of the conference are published by the C.G. Jung Institute of Los Angeles.

Christian Spirituality and the Depth Psychology of C.G. Jung Conference
c/o Sister Ann Cic
Benedictine Monastery
Pecos, NM 87552

The third annual conference was held from June 19 to July 5, 1987 in the Benedictine monastery town of the Black Madonna, Einsiedeln, Switzerland.

Eranos Conference
c/o Rudolf Ritsema
Casa Eranos
CH-6612 Ascona
Switzerland

The **Eranos Conference** was founded in 1933 by Olga Froebe-Kapteyn who invited scholars in the fields of psychology, art, mysticism, etc. Jung figured largely in the early meetings.

"The main aim is to confront and join Jung's striving for 'Know Thyself' with other research such as science of religions, humanities, physics, natural sciences and arts.

The proceedings are published in the **ERANOS-Jahrbücher**, volume 54 of which has just been released." (See #6)

The theme for 1987 is "Crossroads". Some topics are:

"Oedipus Revisited" by James Hillman (psychology)

"Carrefour de l'être, carrefour de la vie" by Dominique Zahan (ethnology)

"Der Ort des Menschen im Nô-Spiel" by Shizuteru Ueda (Buddhism)

Ghost Ranch Conference for Jungian Analysts and Candidates
c/o Chiron Publications
400 Linden Avenue
Wilmette, IL 60091
(312) 256-7551

The 1987 theme was "The Borderline Personality in Analysis".

"Located some sixty miles northwest of Santa Fe, NM, in the lands of the Pueblo Indians, **Ghost Ranch** covers 21,000 acres."

The **Ghost Ranch Conference** is hosted by **Chiron Publications.**

Presentations include:

"Shadow and Self Dynamics in Borderline Cases" by Susanne Kacirek

"Gender and the Borderline" by Andrew Samuels

Harvest
c/o Centerpoint
33 Main Street, #302
Nashua, NH 03060

"**Harvest** is Centerpoint's annual conference held in New Hampshire at the time of the beautiful fall foliage. Noted Jungians, analysts, authors, etc. are speakers for the three-day conference. In the past these have included Joseph and Jane Wheelwright, Philip and Beverley Zabriskie, Edward Edinger, Jean Shinoda Bolen, David Hart and many others."

Images of Transformation
Jungian Retreat in the Swiss Alps
c/o Jan Aycock
Center for International Programs

Batten Arts and Letters, Room 828
Old Dominion University
Norfolk, VA 23508

"High above Montreux, the majestic beauty and tranquility of the Swiss Apls provide the right setting for this unique experience. A seven day off campus retreat integrating several modes of learning will focus on the transcendent dimension of C.G. Jung's philosophy. Using the theme **"Images of Transformation"** and various mythological motifs, retreat activities will explore analogues of experience stimulated by archetypes of transformation."

International Congress
c/o IAAP (International Association for
     Analytical Psychology)
Postfach 115
8042 Zürich
Switzerland

The 10th annual **International Congress** was held in September, 1986, in Berlin. The proceeds are published. (See #9)

Journey Into Wholeness
c/o Jim and Annette Cullipher
21 Windemere Drive
Greenville, SC 29615
(803) 268-3947

"This conference began to fill a personal need - a need to have some time with John Sanford. We (my husband an Episcopal priest and I) could not afford to go to San Diego, so I brought together 50 other people that I thought would like to hear what he had to say and we shared the cost of having him with us for a week. It was such a good experience that we repeated it the next year, but this time we moved from the church to a conference center. This allowed those of us with family to have a time apart. We never intended to develop an ongoing conference but the hunger is great."

The Spring Conference is held at Epworth-by-the-Sea Conference Center ("set in the middle of a stand of large, old, moss-laden live oaks"), St. Simon's Island, GA, and the fall conference is held at **Kanuga,** An Episcopal Center. (See p. 43)

"The purpose and design of this conference is to provide a setting for Christians to explore the concepts of Carl Jung and what they have of value to offer us on our spiritual journey, in discovering who we are through our dreams, journaling, meditation, active imagination, etc.; in living out our lives and relationships in love so as not to project our darkness onto others; in discovering the Christ within and participating in His continuing creation."

Examples are:

"Inner Meanings from the Gospel of St. John" by John Sanford

"Apprenticed to Goodness" by Alan Jones

Jungian Art Therapy Conference
c/o Ethne Gray
112 Chestnut Street
West Newton, MA 02165
(617) 332-0383

The Bi-Annual Conference on **Jungian Art Therapy** is held at the University of New Mexico, Albuquerque, NM.

Jungian Child Analysts Conference
c/o IAAP
Postfach 115
8042 Zürich
Switzerland

The 3rd International Workshop of **Jungian Child Analysts** took place in 1986 in Stroud, England. "The topics were: interpretation in child analysis, problems of different settings, relationship between the therapist and the parents of a child/adolescent."

**The Jungian Winter Seminar
in Zurich, Switzerland**
Five Essex Square
P.O. Box 337
Essex, CT 06426-0337
(203) 767-1620

"**The Jungian Winter Seminars in Switzerland** were first held in 1974, and are now held annually in January. The aim of the seminars is simple: to provide an intensive two-week program of lectures on analytical psychology, in English, for persons with all degrees of sophistication and knowledge of Jungian psychology. To complement the lectures, most of which are delivered by faculty of the **C.G. Jung Institute** in Kusnacht, Switzerland, additional discussion and process sessions are held. No proceedings are published."

The 1988 **Jungian Winter Seminar** preliminary lecture schedule includes:

"The Eternal Child" by Helmut Barz

"Clinical Approaches to the Cinderella Fairy Tale" by Katrin Asper

National Conference of Jungian Analysts
c/o C.G. Jung Institute of Chicago
550 Callan Avenue
Evanston, IL 60202

The C.G. Jung Institute of Chicago will host the September 1987 **National Conference of Jungian Analysts.** The theme will be "The Psychological Impact of American Culture of Analysis."

5 PERIODICALS

Analytische Psychologie
Zeitschrift für Analytische Psychologie
   und ihre Grenzgebiete
S. KARGER AG, Basel
Postfach
CH-4009 Basel
Switzerland

"This journal features articles covering all aspects of C.G. Jung's analytical psychology. It publishes clinical and methodological work as well as psychological statements concerning the modern way of life." Summaries in English.
   Representative articles:
   "Der therapeutische Umgang mit Schattenaspekten der narzisstischen Störung" by K. Asper-Bruggisser
   "Die Sphinx - Symbol am Anfang" by J. Rasche
   Analytische Psychologie also has book reviews, announcements and conference reports. There is a 1969-1985 cumulative index.

Anima
An Experiential Journal
Anima Publications
1053 Wilson Avenue
Chambersburg, PA 17201
(717) 263-8303

Anima was established in 1974 and appears semi-annually. It "concentrates on the quest for wholeness through values traditionally labeled feminine. It values the inner part of the person, the vital principle, the breath of life, the Anima." It publishes articles on feminism, psychology, and religion, as well as poetry. Subjects include "Jung and Teilhard", "Goddesses and mythology", "feminine intuition" and "religion and witchcraft." Contributors include Jean Houston, June Singer and Edward Whitmont.

It also publishes books on Asian religions for teaching and research. For example:

Darśān: Seeing the Divine Image in India by Diana Eck.

It also makes available the publications of the Institute for Advanced Studies of World Religions. For example:

A Buddhist Leader in Ming China: The Life and Thought of Han-shan Te-Ch'ing by Sung-peng Hsu

A cumulative index was published in volume 10.

The Bulletin of Psychological Type. See p. 73.

Cahiers Jungiens de Psychanalyse
1, Place de L'Ecole Militaire
75007 Paris
France

Cahiers Jungiens de Psychanalyse began in the spring of 1974. It is the quarterly journal of the Jungian analysts in France. Each quarter takes up a different theme. The spring issue of 1987 pursued the theme of "L'archétype de l'ombre dans un monde clivé". Representative articles were:

"Ombre Noire - Ombre Blanche" by Martine Gallard-Drahon

"L'Ombre: Pulsion et Représentation" by Susanne Kacirek

The winter 1986 theme was "L'angoisse", and the fall, 1986 theme was "L'espace intérieur".

Chiron
An Annual Review of Jungian Analysis
Chiron Publications
400 Linden Avenue
Wilmette, IL 60091
(312) 256-7551

"Created in 1983, **Chiron** is the first professional Jungian journal in the United States to be specifically clinical in content. Sponsored by the Inter-Regional Society of Jungian Analysts and the Chicago Society of Jungian Analysts, **Chiron's** contributors are Jungian analysts and psychoanalytically oriented therapists with Jungian interests who explore old and new methods for healing the soul."
The 1987 issue centered around "Archetypes in Analysis". The 1986 issue concentrated on "The Body in Analysis.

Gorgo
Zeitschrift für archetypische Psychologie
   und bildhaftes Denken
BSB Buch Service Basel
Postfach
4002 Basel
Switzerland

Gorgo is a bi-annual journal and "was founded by Wolfgang Giegerich in 1979 to give voice to Archetypal Psychology in the German speaking realm.
Gorgo addresses itself to central themes in all lesser or greater areas of our culture and in our personal as well as collectively human existence. Its aim in doing so is to pay special attention to the 'Gorgonian', seemingly or actually hopeless aspects that tend to spellbind and blind us. By reflecting them from an imaginal perspective and in the context of our philosophical, religious, and literary tradition, it tries to deepen them for our understanding

and to connect us with their intrinsic meaning; to uncover our participation in them; and to point to ways of a kind of philosophical coexistence with them."

Gorgo is geared toward analysts and analysands, the general educated public, writers, artists, philosophers, anthropologists, political scientists, cultural critics and theologians.

Harvest
Journal for Jungian Studies
Analytical Psychology Club of London
37 York Street Chambers
York Street
London W1H 1DE
England

Harvest is published annually by the Analytical Psychology Club and has to date had 32 issues. It comes out in the autumn.

"**Harvest** appeals to those who have a serious interest in Jungian Studies, to the mind and the heart. It has an extensive book review section, often articles in themselves, and we have added a section for correspondence. Some of the articles are from lectures given at the Analytical Psychology Club here in London, and the Editor also invites analysts of international reputation to contribute. It has a clinical section."

Among articles in the 1986 issue:
"Gnosis and Psychology" by Gilles Quispel
"A Sonata in the Sand" by Joel Ryce-Menuhin
"The Rescued Child or the Misappropriation of Time - On the Search for Meaning" by Wolfgang Giegerrich

L'IMMAGINALE
Rassegna di psicologia immaginale
Casella Postale 273

73100 LECCE
Italy

L'Immaginale, a bi-annual journal, was established in 1982.
Examples of articles from the April 1987 issue:
"La Presenza nei Sogni" by Anna Benvenuti
"Il Quarto Cavaliere dell'Apocalisse" by Dario V. Caggìa
"Prigioniero della Montagna Incantata" by Maurilio Orbecchi

IAAP Newsletter
International Association for Analytical Psychology
Jef Dehing
Avenue J.B. Depaire 91   **LIMITED**
B 1020 Brussels   **CIRCULATION**
Belgium

The **IAAP Newsletter** publishes reports on the activities of professional Jungian societies around the world. It also carries an extensive bibliography of publications by Jungian analysts. (See #8)

In Touch Newsletter. See p. 36.

Inward Light
Friends Conference on Religion and Psychology
3518 Bradley Lane
Washington, DC 20015

The Journal of Analytical Psychology
The Society of Analytical Psychology Ltd.
1 Daleham Gardens
London NW3
England
    orders:
Journals Marketing Department
Academic Press, Inc. (London) Ltd.

24-28 Oval Road
London NW1 7DX
England

"**The Journal of Analytical Psychology,** founded
in 1955 under the editorship of Michael Fordham, is
sponsored and edited by The Society of Analytical
Psychology in London, and published by Academic
Press. It is the first and still one of the main publications on analytical psychology in the English language. The principal aim of this journal is to disseminate the thoughts, theories and clinical work of C.G.
Jung as well as the developments of his ideas as they
occur and are being worked out in England and in
all other countries by analytical psychologists and by
those interested in analytical psychology. It also
draws on contributions that explore the links of analytical psychology with the arts, anthropology, religion, philosophy, biology and physics. The **Journal**
thus aims to be a stimulating international and interdisciplinary forum for discussion, comments and de-
bates. Emphasis is, however, laid on collating theory
with clinical practice and research.
    Besides the major articles the **Journal** includes:
    comments in relation to papers and points of view
published in the **Journal**
    short notes which communicate seminal clinical
or theoretical ideas that may inspire novel lines of
thought and research
    correspondence
    an extensive review section of books and articles
    short summaries of 'Books Received'
    'Journal Reviews' of papers published in other
journals by members of the International Association
for Analytical Psychology
    biographical notes of the authors concerned in
each issue of the **Journal**
    bibliographical list of the **Collected Works** of C.G.
Jung"

Examples of papers:
"Healing and wounding: the collision of the sacred and the profane in narcissism" by C. Savitz
"Dreams of the Yolngu aborigines of Australia" by L. Petchkovsky and J. Cawte

Journal of Psychological Type. See p. 74.

Junguīana
Revista da Sociedade Brasileira de
    Psicologia Analītica
Soceidade Brasileira de Psicologia Analītica
04008 - Rua Livramento, 133
Sao Paulo, Brazil
02240 - R. Almirante Pereira Guimaraes 72
    CJ 504/505
Rio de Janeiro, Brazil

The **Junguīana** is published by the Sociedade Brasileira de Psycologia Analītica annually, and the last issue was #4.
Sample of recent articles:
""Ademus" - A psicologia da Inveja e Sua Funçao no Processo Criativo: Um Estudo di Psicologia Simbō-lica" by Carlos Byington
"Psicoterapia e Alquimia" by Edward Edinger
There are English abstracts.

Das Menschenbild
Die Zeitschrift für Selbstverwirklichung
    und Persönlichkeitsentfaltung
Anthropos
Forschungs-Institut
Pfarrgässli 5
CH-6060 SARNEN
Switzerland

"The Institute was founded in 1984 under the leadership of Walter Odermatt, a psychologist of the

Jung-Institute and a theologian. A quarterly magazine
Das Menschenbild has now reached the 15th issue.
A group of scientists from different disciplines have
joined together for a cooperative work. While remain-
ing true to the method and discipline of their own
scientific research, they endeavor to communicate
their insight in the light of our present life and in
a language which is understood by everybody."
Themes of recent issues:
"Das Wesen der Meditation"
"Die Träume"
The Institute also publishes the "Anthropos Stu-
dienreihe", a report with 6 talks of the annual sym-
posium (1985) in Herisau entitled, "Education at the
Crossroads".
There is also a meditation course of 6 tapes in
German called "Holistic Meditation".
We envision reaching ordinary people who have
a lively interest in these questions.

Parabola
The Magazine of Myth and Tradition
656 Broadway
New York, NY 10012-2317

Parabola is a quarterly magazine featuring "contemporary fiction, essays, interviews, traditional folk
tales, and reviews of relevant books, films and exhi-
bitions" geared to insight into essential questions of
the human mind and spirit. The themes of its issues
have included: "Inner Alchemy", "Androgeny", "The
Night and the Hermit", and "Memory and Forgetting",
with contributions by Joseph Campbell, Mircea
Eliade, Peter Matthiessen, and so forth.
Parabola also offers several books including:
Leaning on the Moment: Interviews from **Parabola**
Magazine
And There Was Light: The Autobiography of
Jacques Lusseyran

Per Immagini
Rivista-seminario internazionale 'secondo'
  psicologia-imaginale
Alleanza per la Fondazione Individuale
Via dello Stracchino, 25
50065 Pontassieve, FI
Italy

Per Immagini is "the official publication of Alleanza per la Fondazione Individuale, an association which was founded to encourage a new, diverse humanistic space-movement starting from the core of the contemporary anthropological-cultural crisis. It is in fact the official publication of the Alleanza through its psychological institution for imaginary-research."

Some article examples:
"The Song of the Threshold" by Giorgio Concato
"In-Sight" by Gianluca Montani

Psychological Perspectives
A Semi-Annual Review of Jungian Thought
10349 West Pico Blvd.
Los Angeles, CA 90064
(213) 556-1193

Psycological Perspectives deals with:
"the collective unconscious: the world and its people, its issues and its ideas from a Jungian perspective

fairy tales, art, religion, mythology, and literature explored psychologically

personal essays of depth, warmth and sometimes wit

books and films reviewed with an eye and an ear to their archetypal themes"

It is published twice yearly. Highlights from the spring 1987 issue:

"Mind-Body Healing Comes of Age" by Norman

Cousins
  "Psychological Impact of Psychic Abilities" by
Russell Targ and Arthur Hastings
  "Healing the Psyche, Healing the Earth" by Jean
Shinoda Bolen

Quadrant
Journal of the C.G. Jung Foundation for
  Analytical Psychology
28 East 39th Street
New York, NY 10016
(212) 697-6430

  "Quadrant, a twice-yearly journal, presents lively
articles, commentaries, and reviews examining mythology, religion and philosophy, symbolism and literature, social sciences, and clinical practice in a
uniquely focused light. Addressing contemporary ideas
and problems from the perspective of Jungian psychology, **Quadrant** explores the growth of Jungian
thought and its relation to the psychological realities
of individuals and society today."
  Articles from the Fall 1986 issue:
  "Aggression: A Jungian Point of View" by Richmond K. Greene
  "Hephaestus: Model of New-Age Masculinity" by
Irene Gad

Rivista di Psicologia Analytica
Via Gallonia n. 8
00161 Roma
Italy

The San Francisco Jung Institute Library Journal. See
#8.

Shim-Song Yon-Gu
Korean Society for Analytical Psychology
Room no. 6633

Dept. of Neuropsychiatry
Seoul National University Hospital
28 Yongundong, Chonnogu
Seoul 110 Korea

Shim-Song Yon-Gu is a twice-yearly newsletter in Korean.

Spring
An Annual of Archetypal Psychology
    and Jungian Thought
Spring Publications
P.O. Box 222069
Dallas, TX 75222

Spring is "the only international yearbook in the field - since 1941 - blending original scholarship, psychotherapeutic and archetypal imagination. New directions in understanding dreams, syndromes, and psychosomatic disorders; historical and biographical research on C.G. Jung; critical examination of basic Jungian ideas; post-Jungian controversy; works-in-progress." (See #6.)
    Recent articles include:
    "Psychological Projection and the Magic Lantern" by L.W. Bailey
    "Psychic Wounds and Body Scars" by Rose-Emily Rothenberg
    "Horses with Wings" by Denise Levertov

The Type Reporter. See p. 77.

6 BOOK PUBLISHERS

Chiron Publications
400 Linden Avenue
Wilmette, IL 60091

Chiron is the publisher of **Chiron:** An Annual Review of Jungian Analysis. (See p. 87) Among the books they publish are:
The Springs of Creativity: The Bible and the Creative Process of the Psyche by Heinz Westman
Jung's Treatment of Christianity: The Psychotherapy of a Religious Tradition by Murray Stein

Consulting Psychologists Press. See p. 74-75.

Crossroad Publication Co.
370 Lexington Avenue
New York, NY
(212) 532-3650

Among the Jungian-oriented books they publish are:
Jung and Christianity: The Challenge of Reconciliation by Wallace B. Clift
Prophetic Ministry: The Psychology and Spirituality of Pastoral Care by Morton T. Kelsey

Daimon Press
AM Klosterplatz
CH-8840 Einsiedeln
Switzerland

Daimon Press offers publications in psychology,

philosophy and religious history. Many of their authors have given papers at Eranos.

Examples of books are:

Symbolic and Clinical Approaches in Theory and Practice, Collected essays of the Jungian International Congress in Jerusalem, 1983

Aus C.G. Jungs letzten Jahren by Aniela Jaffé

Meetings with Jung by E.A. Bennet

Kunst und schöpferisches Unbewusstes by Erich Neumann

Dallas Institute. For publications see p. 51.

Eranos-Jahrbücher
Casa Eranos
CH-6612 ASCONA
Switzerland

The **ERANOS-Jahrbücher** makes available the more than 50 volumes of the Eranos lectures. (See p. 80-81.)

The 1984 edition of the **ERANOS Yearbook** pursued the theme of "Beauty of the World" and some articles included:

"Science and Art: Complementary Views of Human Experience" by Victor Weisskopf

"Visage et défigurations de la Beauté" by Jean Brun

"Die Welt als Wirklichkeit und Gleichnis im Buddhismus Zentralasiens" by Hans-Joachim Klimkeit

"**Princeton University Press** (see below) has published 6 volumes of selections from the **ERANOS-yearbooks,** and **Spring Publications** (see below) have also published several extracts."

Falcon Press
3660 North 3rd Street
Phoenix, AZ 85012
(602) 246-3546

Falcon Press publishes "The Jungian Series", which include:
Jungian Analysts: Their Visions and Vulnerabilities edited by J. Marvin Spiegelman and Joseph McNair
Buddhism and Jungian Psychology by J. Marvin Spiegelman and Mokusen Miyuki
They also put out a "Jungian Psycho-Mythology Series" written by J. Marvin Spiegelman.

Guild for Psychological Studies Publishing House
2230 Divisadero Street
San Francisco, CA 94115

"For over 40 years the **Guild for Psychological Studies** (see p. 20-21) has offered seminars on the process of becoming value-centered individuals. The **Publishing House of the Guild,** established in 1984, will continue to make available to a larger audience the life-serving ideas worked with in seminars."
Sample titles:
Intersection and Beyond by Elizabeth Boyden Howes
A Trilogy called **Thunder in the Roots** by Sheila Moon:
Knee-Deep in Thunder
Hunt Down the Prize
Deepest Roots

The Guild of Pastoral Psychology
37 Hogarth Hill
London NW11 6AY
England

The Guild of Pastoral Psychology (see p. 66) publishes a large series of pamphlets and cassettes from their lecture series. Titles include:
"The Problem of Contact with the Animus" by Barbara Hannah
"Christianity Within" by Toni Wolff

"Analyst at the Cross Roads" by A. Plaut
"The Problem of Authority in the Early Develop-
ment of the Individual" by Kenneth Lambert
"Physics and Psyche" by C.D. Curling

Inner City Books
Studies in Jungian Psychology by Jungian Analysts
Box 1271, Station Q
Toronto, Canada M4T 2P4

"**Inner City Books** was founded in 1980 to promote
the understanding and practical application of the
work of C.G. Jung." Their books include:
The Owl Was a Baker's Daughter: Obesity, Ano-
rexia Nervosa and the Repressed Feminine by Marion
Woodman
Descent to the Goddess: A Way of Initiation for
Women by Sylvia Brinton Perera
Addiction to Perfection: The Still Unravished Bride
by Marion Woodman
The Pregnant Virgin. A Process of Psychological
Transformation by Marion Woodman
The Spiral Way: A Woman's Healing Journey by
Aldo Carotenuto
The Jungian Experience: Analysis and Individuation
by James A. Hall
Phallos: Sacred Image of Masculinity by Eugene
Monick

H. Karnac Books Ltd.
58 Gloucester Road
London SW7 4QY
England

Karnac Books publishes and distributes the **Library
of Analytical Psychology** series for the Society of
Analytical Psychology of London.
The titles of the **Library of Analytical Psychology**
are:

Vol. 7: Explorations of the Self
Vol. 6: My Self, My Many Selves
Vol. 5: Analysis, Repair and Individuation
Vol. 4: Dying and Creating: A Search for Meaning
Vol. 3: The Self and Autism
Vol. 2: Technique in Jungian Analysis
Vol. 1: Analytical Psychology: A Modern Science

The Open Door Inc.
P.O. Box 855
Charlottesville, VA 22902
(804) 293-5068

Their books include:
Prayer and Temperament: Different Prayer Forms for Different Personality Types by Chester P. Michael and Marie C. Norrisey
Arise: A Christian Psychology of Love by Chester P. Michael and Marie C. Norrisey
Their audio tape cassettes include:
Call to Wholeness and Holiness, 6 hours of tapes
Jungian Psychology and Religion, 6 hours of tapes
They also publish **The Open Door:** A Quarterly Publication on Spirituality and Prayer

Paulist Press
977 MacArthur Blvd.
Mahwah, NJ 07430
(201) 825-7300

Books they publish include:
From Image to Likeness: A Jungian Path in the Gospel Journey by W. Harold Grant, Magdala Thompson and Thomas E. Clarke
Spiritual Pilgrims: Carl Jung and Teresa of Avila by John Welch

Princeton University Press
41 William Street
Princeton, NJ 08540

Princeton University Press publishes **The Bollingen Series,** which began in 1943 and is named after the village where Carl Jung had his tower. It was established by Paul and Mary Mellon. "The idea of the collected works of Jung might be considered the central core, the binding factor, not only of the Foundation's general direction, but also of the ultimate intellectual temper of **Bollingen's** series as a whole." The series includes original works, translations and new editions. The story of the **Bollingen** Foundation is told in **An Adventure in Collecting the Past** by William McGuire.

It includes Jung's **Collected Works** in English (see #9) and many other classics in Jungian psychology, including:
The Living Symbol by Gerhard Adler
The Origin and History of Consciousness by Erich Neumann
The Great Mother by Erich Neumann
Psychic Energy by M. Esther Harding

Routledge & Kegan Paul
Division of Methuen, Inc.
29 West 35th Street
New York, NY 10001-2291
(212) 244-3336

Routledge & Kegan Paul publishes titles of interest to a Jungian audience:
Jung and the Post-Jungians by Andrew Samuels
The Dream Body in Relationships: Dreambody, Anthropos, and Hologram Aspects of Couples, Families and Groups by Arnold Mindell

Shambhala Publications
314 Dartmouth Street
Boston, MA 02116

Some Jungian titles are:
On Dreams and Death: A Jungian Interpretation
by Marie-Louise von Franz
On the Way to the Wedding: Transforming the
Love Relationship by Linda Schierse Leonard
Jungian Analysis edited by Murray Stein

Sigo Press
77 North Washington Street, #201
Boston, MA 02114

"**Sigo Press** publishes books which continue the
work of C.G. Jung and explore human growth and
development from a Jungian perspective." Some titles
are:
Puer Aeternus: A Psychological Study of the Adult
Struggle with the Paradise of Childhood by Marie-
Louise von Franz
The Unconscious in its Empirical Manifestations
by C.A. Meier
The Longing for Paradise by Mario Jacoby
The Death of a Woman by Jane Hollister Wheel-
wright
The Grail Legend by Emma Jung and Marie-Louise
von Franz

Spring Publications, Inc.
P.O. Box 222069
Dallas, TX 75222
(214) 943-4093

Spring (see p. 95) is one of the largest Jungian
book publishers. They list their books under the following headings: Jungian & Archetypal Psychology;
Psychotherapy; Fairytales & Symbolism; Mythology

& Classics; Psychology & Religion
   Some of the titles are:
   Anima as Fate by Cornelia Brunner
   Archetypal Psychology by James Hillman
   Animus and Anima by Emma Jung
   Power in the Helping Professions by Adolf Gug-
genbühl-Craig
   The Self in Psychotic Process by John Weir Perry
   Hermes: Guide of Souls by Karl Kerényi

Tools for Inner Growth
Box 520
Chiloquin, OR 97624

   See the back pages for ordering information on
our current titles.

7 MAIL ORDER
BOOK SOURCES

Analytical Psychology Society of
  Western New York, Inc.
166 Cleveland Avenue
Buffalo, NY 14222
(716) 885-1138 or 882-0446

The **Analytical Psychology Society of Western New York** has a book service of over 200 titles and more than 30 cassette tapes.

Anna's Gate
204 Hill Street
Galena, IL 61036

"We have a full service bookstore, plus mail order business. We specialize in all facets of Jungian psychology, mythology, folk literature and Jungian related subjects."

Banyen Books
2685 West Broadway
Vancouver, B.C. V6K 2G2
Canada

Banyen Books has a computer print-out list of close to 300 books in their Jungian section.

Centerpoint
33 Main Street, #302
Nashua, NH 03060

Centerpoint offers around 100 Jungian-oriented titles at a 10% discount.

C.G. Jung Bookstore
10349 West Pico Boulevard
Los Angeles, CA 90064
(213) 556-1196

The **C.G. Jung Bookstore** in Los Angeles has a catalog covering a wide range of over 400 Jungian-oriented titles in the areas of: Alchemy, Astrology & Occult Matters; Dream Studies; Folklore & Fairy Tales; Child Studies; Symbolism, and so forth.
They also have a special annotated section of "New & Notable Titles".

C.G. Jung Institute of Chicago Bookstore
550 Callan Avenue
Evanston, IL 60202
(312) 475-4848

"The Bookstore of the **C.G. Jung Institute** stocks more than 2,000 titles on analytical psychology and related subjects, such as mythology, dreams, fairy tales, art and art therapy, religion, philosophy, women's studies, and the emerging subject of men's studies."
"We are glad to take a phone or mail order. Write to **Bookstore,** use the order form from the catalogue or **Book News.**"

C.G. Jung Book Service
28 East 39th Street
New York, NY 10016-2587
(212) 697-6433

"The **C.G. Jung Book Service** has an annotated catalogue of books on Jungian Studies and those subjects which influenced C.G. Jung. The annotations are brief, but concise, and the selections reflect the wide range of categories which intersect with Jungian Studies offered by the **Book Service**, categories such as Psychology, Anthropology, Mythology, Astrology, Literature, Mysticism, Philosophy, Eastern Studies, Art and Religion." They carry close to 400 titles.

H. Karnac Books Ltd.
58 Gloucester Road
London SW7 4QY
England

"We always have ample stock of Jungian titles starting from the **Collected Works** and keeping our list of titles up to date as much as possible." They carry over 200 titles in analytical psychology.

Yes! Bookshop
1035 31st Street N.W.
Washington, DC 20007-4482
(202) 338-2727

Yes! Bookshop sells the catalog **Jungian Psychology**, A Comprehensive Guide for $2.50. It is an annotated bibliography of about 250 Jungian books.

8 LIBRARIES AND
BIBLIOGRAPHIC TOOLS

MAJOR JUNGIAN RESEARCH LIBRARIES

"The Archive for Research in Archetypal Symbolism (ARAS) is a unique collection of pictures and scholarly material devoted to the study of symbolic imagery. It is an important instrument for discerning the power and purpose of these enduring symbols as they are expressed in the course of history.

The **Archive** consists of photographs of works of art, ritual images, and artifacts, cross-indexed and organized chronologically from ancient times to the present. Each picture is mounted and accompanied by text prepared by professional researchers and consultants.

A project is now underway to re-format existing material and develop new areas of research toward a first-stage core of 10,000 images. The **Archive** is particularly strong in the areas of Prehistoric, Ancient Near Eastern, Egyptian, Greco-Roman, and Christian art. Research is currently expanding into Asian, Jewish, Islamic, African, Oceanic, and Native American traditions. Computerization and laser disk technology will provide enhanced accessibility to the **Archive.**

ARAS welcomes the interested public as well as students and specialists in a variety of disciplines including psychology, anthropology, archaeology, art history, religion and philosophy. The **Archive** has long been recognized as a valuable resource for tracing images appearing in dreams as well as the relation-

ships among symbols in myth, legend, and all other
forms of human creative endeavor."
    Collections are housed at:
    The C.G. Jung Institute of New York
    The C.G. Jung Institute of Los Angeles
    The C.G. Jung Institute of San Francisco

Kristine Mann Library
C.G. Jung Center
28 East 39th Street
New York, NY 10016
(212) 697-7877

"The **Analytical Psychology Club** founded and
maintains the **Kristine Mann Library,** named for Dr.
Mann, one of the earliest practitioners of analytical
psychology in the United States. Her bequest to the
Club of 400 books, received in 1945, formed the
nucleus from which the **Library's** permanent collection
has grown by means of carefully selected gifts and
purchases. The **Library** is the main repository of
materials related to analytical psychology and contains many rare items. It includes all of C.G. Jung's
works published in English and German from 1902 to
date and also works by specialists in analytical psychology and related materials in the fields of religion, philosophy, art, anthropology, mythology, fairy
tales and alchemy. The author/title catalogue includes
approximately 19,000 entries. There are 6,000 volumes and 2,343 file items and the collection continues to grow.
    The **Library** is located on the fourth floor of the
C.G. Jung Center. A professional librarian is on hand
to assist researchers and orient visitors to the collection."
    "The **Library's** card catalog was published in book
form by G.K. Hall & Co. (Boston) in 1978 and provides detailed author and subject analysis of the
Library's holdings."

C.G. Jung Institute of Chicago Library
550 Callan Avenue
Evanston, IL 60202
(312) 475-4848

"**The Institute Library** houses over 2,500 volumes, with concentrations in analytical psychology, psychoanalysis, folklore, and myth (and supplemental holdings in art, literature, women's studies, and religion). There are also collections of several periodicals, including **Anima, Chiron, Harvest, The Journal of Analytical Psychology, Parabola, The Psychoanalytic Study of the Child, Psychological Perspectives, Quadrant,** and **Spring.**
Members are entitled to sign out any circulating materials except current reserve items. Members and non-members alike are welcome to use the **Library** in-house during **Institute** hours. Assistance is available in locating research materials and preparing bibliographies.
We have a list of vertical file items, which are all uncatalogueable pamphlets, monographs, photocopies of articles, etc. They currently number 250+. We are in the process of indexing all of the Jungian periodicals listed in our **Library** description by putting them on our computer. When this is finished we will be able to generate bibliographies by author/title. Subject indexing will be the next step, although we expect that to take another 18 months. We are also investigating the possibility of interconnecting by computer the libraries of several institutes, thereby providing access to research materials and augmenting each library's ability to provide a depth of resources."

The Max and Lore Zeller Library
C.G. Jung Institute of Los Angeles
10349 West Pico Boulevard
Los Angeles, CA 90064

"The Max and Lore Zeller Library at the Institute has the finest collection of Jungian literature in Southern California and is a rich resource for information on Analytical Psychology and related subjects."

The Virginia Allan Detloff Library
C.G. Jung Institute of San Francisco
2040 Gough Street
San Francisco, CA 94109
(415) 771-8055

"The Virginia Allan Detloff Library has a collection of over 5,000 books and periodicals, 800 cassette tapes, and a large file of unpublished papers. Reflecting the wide range of Jung's interests, the Library acquires works not only in analytical psychology, but also in art, mythology, philosophy and religion East and West, literature, alchemy and the occult, folklore and fairy tales. Works in mainstream psychology, psychiatry and psychoanalysis are also collected to provide a context for the integration of Jung's views with other contemporary clinical thought.

Borrowers include analysts of the Institute, candidates in training, staff, clinic interns, and, by invitation, local scholars and long-time donors. Advanced students and researchers, and others with special Jungian topics who cannot locate materials elsewhere, use the Library on site by special arrangement with the Librarian."

C.G. Jung-Institut Zürich Library
Hornweg 28
8700 Küsnacht
Switzerland

In addition to a large collection of books the Zürich Library has small but growing video collections and a picture archive of over 2,000 pictures by

Jung's patients and others. It also has specialized bibliographies and a Jungian Journal Index.

Isabel Briggs Myers Memorial Library
CAPT (Center for Applications of Psychological Type)
2720 N.W. 6th Street
Gainesville, FL 32609

See p. 73 for information on the **Isabel Briggs Myers Memorial Library.**

BIBLIOGRAPHIC TOOLS

BOOKS

Reading Lists. See #9.

New Book Acquisitions - C.G. Jung Library, Zürich. A list is published twice annually. The October 1986-March 1987 list contains over 200 titles.

The San Francisco Jung Institute Library Journal, a quarterly, "is the first Jungian publication devoted exclusively to reviews. It looks deeply into current books, movies, art exhibitions, music and other events. From the death of Mae West to the latest psychoanalytic perspectives on narcissism, the subjects covered by the **Library Journal** have been arresting and illuminating. A number of new Jungian voices have been heard, sharing their understanding and appreciation of different areas of experience from fresh perspectives."

C.G. Jung and Analytical Psychology: A Comprehensive Bibliography by Joseph F. Vincie and Margreta Rathbauer-Vincie. This is the "first complete international bibliography related to both Jung and the Jungian School of Thought. Entries include approximately 4,000 books and articles and over 800 reviews in every major European language and in chronological order from before 1916 through the end of 1975."

Jung and Theology: A Bibliographical Essay by James W. Heisig. This is a comprehensive listing up to August 1972. This essay "will attempt to set forth in a systematic fashion the literature available on the topic "Jung and theology", and to sketch the broad outlines of its achievements." 442 items are listed.

Bibliographies are available from the **Virginia Allan Detloff Library** at the **C.G. Jung Institute of San Francisco** (up to November 1984). They are listed under the following headings:

Basic reading list - Zürich; Basic reading list - San Francisco (see #9); Analytic technique; Antisemitism and Jung; Borderline patients, by John Beebe; Cancer; Child development, developed from the collection of Florence Grossenbacher; Cross-cultural issues; Death and dying, by Barbara Jeskalian, San Jose State University Library; Dreams (1) Reference works for amplification of dream symbols (2) An annotated bibliography for use in amplification research, by Marilyn Nagy; Dreams and illness; Dreams and fiction, a checklist, by Lee Zimmerman and Carolyn Hoche; Drugs - Some drugs that cause reactions; Greek goddesses, by Jean Shinoda Bolen; Group psychotherapy, by Crittenden Brookes; Holocaust, by Barbara Jeskalian, San Jose State University Library; Myth, symbol and ritual by Barbara Jeskalian, San Jose State University Library; Nuclear conflict, psychological aspects of; Orthomolecular psychiatry and counseling; Outline of the Jungian model, by Peter Rutter; Psyche-soma relationship; Puer aeternus: Ten ways of looking at the puer, an annotated bibliography by Frederic Wiedemann; Religion and depth psychology, by Barbara Jeskalian, San Jose

State University Library; Sandplay - Selected annotated bibliography by Clare Thompson and Paul Wiltse, photocopied from the book Sandplay studies; Schizophrenia, a selected bibliography by Peter Rutter; Shakespeare's works, related material in the Library's collection; Symbolism; Transpersonal psychology, by Arthur Hastings; Typology; Women.

Volume 20 of the **Collected Works** of C.G. Jung is an Index.

C.G. Jung Seminar Notes has an **Index to Dreams and Visions Seminars,** as well as an **Index to Zarathustra.**

Critical Dictionary of Jungian Analysis by Andrew Samuels, Bani Shorter and Fred Plaut. "The **Dictionary** includes explanations of terms and ideas introduced and developed by Jung, as well as ordinary terms that Jung used in new, unexpected ways."

Diploma Theses. The major training **Institutes** often have a diploma thesis as part of their requirements. For example, 30 or more are produced in Zürich each year.

The Myers-Briggs Type Indicator Bibliography. "This computer-generated listing with author index is prepared and maintained by **CAPT.** It is updated February and August of each year. The February 1986 edition contains over 1,100 listings."

PERIODICALS

Spring has an Index: 1941-1979 by Virginia Detloff. "The **Index** incorporates both an author and subject index as well as the original Table of Contents from each past edition of the annual."

Analytische Psychologie has a 1969-1985 cumulative

index.

Anima has an index in volume 10.

The Journal of Analytical Psychology has a 1955-1984 index.

IAAP Newsletter (see p. 89) has an extensive bibliography of annual article and book publications reported by Jungian professional societies around the world. Issue number 7 reports 1985 data in English, Italian, German, French, Dutch and Portuguese.

9 BASIC READING LIST
AND FILMS

This **Basic Reading List** has been prepared by the **Virginia Allan Detloff Library** of the **C.G. Jung** Institute of San Francisco. The **Jung Institute of Zürich** has a much more extensive reading list available in English, German and Italian.

Elementary or Introductory Works

Bennet, E.A. **What Jung Really Said.** New York: Schocken Books, 1966.

Corrie, Joan. **ABC of Jung's Psychology.** New York: Frank-Maurice, 1927.

Cox, David. **Modern Psychology:** The Teaching of Carl Gustav Jung. New York: Barnes and Noble, 1968.

Dry, Avis M. **Psychology of Jung:** A Critical Interpretation. New York: Wiley, 1961.

Evans, Richard I. **Jung on Elementary Psychology:** A Discussion Between C.G. Jung and Richard Evans. New York: E.P. Dutton, 1976.

Fordham, Frieda. **An Introduction to Jung's Psychology.** Baltimore: Penguin Books, 1953.

Groesbeck, C. Jess. "Carl Jung." Photocopied from **Comprehensive Textbook of Psychiatry, IV.** 1984, pp. 433-440.

Hall, Calvin S. and Vernon J. Nordby. **A Primer of Jungian Psychology.** New York: New American Library, 1973.

Jacobi, Jolande. **The Psychology of C.G. Jung:** An Introduction with Illustrations. 8th ed. New Haven:

Yale Univ. Press, 1973.
Progoff, Ira. **Jung's Psychology and Its Social Meaning**: An Introductory Statement of C.G. Jung's Psychological Theories and a First Interpretation of Their Significance for the Social Sciences. New York: Julian Press, 1953.

Biographies

Bennet, E.A. **C.G. Jung.** London: Barrie and Rockliff, 1961.
Brome, Vincent. **Jung.** New York: Atheneum, 1978.
Hannah, Barbara. **Jung: His Life and Work.** New York: G.P. Putnam's Sons, 1976.
Van der Post, Laurens. **Jung and the Story of Our Time.** New York: Pantheon, 1975.
Wehr, Gerhard. **Portrait of Jung: An Illustrated Biography.** New York: Herder and Herder, 1971.

Works by Jung

The **Collected Works** of C.G. Jung (see next section) contains most of Jung's writings. Some of his work is published in individual volumes as well, and many are in paperback. The following are of unusual interest:

C.G. Jung: Word and Image. Ed. by Aniela Jaffe. Princeton: Princeton Univ. Press, 1979.
Jung, Carl Gustav. **Letters.** Selected and edited by Gerhard Adler. Princeton: Princeton Univ. Press, 1973. 2 vols.
Jung, Carl Gustav. **Man and His Symbols,** by Carl G. Jung, Marie-Louise von Franz, Joseph L. Henderson, Jolande Jacobi, Aniela Jaffe. London: Aldus Books, 1964.
Jung, Carl Gustav. **Memories, Dreams, Reflections.** New York: Pantheon, 1963.
Jung, Carl Gustav. **The Portable Jung.** Ed. by Joseph

Campbell. New York: Viking Press, 1971.

Jung, Carl Gustav. **Psyche and Symbol:** A Selection from the Writings of C.G. Jung. Garden City, NY: Doubleday, 1958.

Jung, Carl Gustav. **Psychological Reflections:** An Anthology of the Writings of C.G. Jung. New York: Pantheon, 1953. Also Princeton Univ. Press, 1953.

Other Basic Works on Analytical Psychology

Adler, Gerhard. **Studies in Analytical Psychology.** New York: W.W. Norton, 1948.

Bertine, Eleanor. **Human Relationships in the Family, in Friendship, in Love.** New York: Longmans, Green, 1958.

Castillejo, Irene Claremont de. **Knowing Woman: A Feminine Psychology.** New York: Harper Colophon Books, 1973.

Edinger, Edward F. **Ego and Archetype:** Individuation and the Religious Function of the Psyche. New York: G.P. Putnam's Sons, 1972.

Fordham, Michael. **Jungian Psychotherapy:** A Study in Analytical Psychology. London: Routledge and Kegan Paul, 1957.

Fordham, Michael. **New Developments in Analytical Psychology.** London: Routledge and Kegan Paul, 1957.

Fordham, Michael. **The Objective Psyche.** London: Routledge and Kegan Paul, 1958.

Fordham, Michael, ed. **Contact with Jung:** Essays on the Influence of His Work and Personality. London: Tavistock Publications, 1963.

Franz, Marie-Louise von. **C.G. Jung: His Myth in Our Time.** New York: G.P. Putnam's Sons, 1975.

Franz, Marie-Louise von. **Individuation in Fairytales.** Zurich: Spring Publications, 1977.

Franz, Marie-Louise von. **An Introduction to the Interpretation of Fairy Tales.** Zurich: Spring Publications, 1970.

Franz, Marie-Louise von. **An Introduction to the Psychology of Fairy Tales.** 4th ed. Irving, TX: Spring Publications, 1970.

Franz, Marie-Louise von. **The Problem of the Puer Aeternus.** Zurich: Spring Publications, 1970. Also Santa Monica, CA: Sigo Press, 1981.

Franz, Marie-Louise von. **Shadow and Evil in Fairy Tales.** Zurich: Spring Publications, 1974.

Guggenbuhl-Craig, Adolf. **Power in the Helping Professions.** New York: Spring Publications, 1971.

Hall, James. **Clinical Uses of Dreams:** Jungian Interpretations and Enactments. New York: Grune and Stratton, 1977.

Hall, James. **Jungian Dream Interpretation:** A Handbook of Theory and Practice. Toronto: Inner City Books, 1983.

Hannah, Barbara. **Striving Towards Wholeness.** New York: G.P. Putnam's Sons, 1971.

Harding, M. Esther. **The "I" and the "Not-I":** A Study in the Development of Consciousness. New York: Pantheon, 1965.

Harding, M. Esther. **Journey Into Self.** New York: David McKay, 1956.

Harding, M. Esther. **The Parental Image:** Its Injury and Reconstruction: A Study in Analytical Psychology. New York: G.P. Putnam's Sons, 1965.

Harding, M. Esther. **Psychic Energy:** Its Source and Its Transformation. Princeton: Princeton Univ. Press, 1947. Also New York: Pantheon, 1947, 1963.

Harding, M. Esther. **The Way of All Women.** New York: G.P. Putnam's Sons, 1970.

Harding, M. Esther. **Woman's Mysteries, Ancient and Modern:** A Psychological Interpretation of the Feminine Principle as Portrayed in Myth, Story and Dreams. New York: Pantheon, 1955. Also London, Longmans, Green, 1935 and New York: G.P. Putnam's Sons, 1971.

Henderson, Joseph L. **Cultural Attitudes in Psy-**

chological Perspective. Toronto, Canada: Inner City Books, 1984.

Henderson, Joseph L. Thresholds of Initiation. Middletown, CT: Wesleyan Univ. Press, 1967, 1979.

Hillman, James. The Dream and the Underworld. New York: Harper & Row, 1979.

Hillman, James. Emotion: A Comprehensive Phenomenology of Theories and Their Meanings for Therapy. Evanston, IL: Northwestern Univ. Press, 1961.

Hillman, James. Loose Ends: Primary Papers in Archetypal Psychology. Zurich: Spring Publications, 1975.

Hillman, James. The Myth of Analysis: Three Essays in Archetypal Psychology. Evanston, IL: Northwestern Univ. Press, 1972.

Hillman, James. Re-Visioning Psychology. New York: Harper & Row, 1975.

Hillman, James. Suicide and the Soul. New York: Harper & Row, 1964.

Homans, Peter. Jung in Context. Chicago: Univ. Of Chicago Press, 1979.

International Congress for Analytical Psychology Proceedings:

    1st, 1958: Current Trends in Analytical Psychology.

    2nd, 1962: The Archetype.

    3rd, 1968: The Reality of the Psyche.

    4th, 1971: The Analytic Process: Aims, Analysis, Training.

    5th, 1974: Success and Failure in Analysis.

    7th, 1980: Methods of Treatment in Analytical Psychology.

    8th, 1982. Money, Food, Drink and Fashion and Depth Dimensions of Physical Existence.

    9th, 1983: Symbolical and Clinical Approaches in Theory and Practice.

Jacobi, Jolande. Complex, Archetype, Symbol in the Psychology of C.G. Jung. New York: Pantheon

Books, 1959.

Jacobi, Jolande. **The Way of Individuation.** New York: Harcourt, Brace & World, 1967.

Jaffe, Aniela. **From the Life and Work of C.G. Jung.** New York: Harper Colophon Books, 1971.

Jung, Emma. **Animus and Anima.** New York: Analytical Psychology Club of New York, 1957.

Kalff, Dora M. **Sandplay: Mirror of a Child's Psyche.** San Francisco: Browser Press, 1971. Also revised edition: **Sandplay: A Psychotherapeutic Approach to the Psyche.** Santa Monica, CA: Sigo Press, 1980.

Library of Analytical Psychology. For the titles of the 7 volumes see p. 100.

McGuire, William, ed. **The Freud/Jung Letters:** The Correspondence Between Sigmund Freud and C.G. Jung. Princeton: Princeton Univ. Press, 1974.

Mattoon, Mary Ann. **Applied Dream Analysis: A Jungian Approach.** New York: John Wiley, 1978. Revised edition published as **Understanding Dreams,** Dallas: Spring Publications, 1984.

Mattoon, Mary Ann. **Jungian Psychology in Perspective.** London: The Free Press, 1981.

Neumann, Erich. **The Child:** Structure and Dynamics of the Nascent Personality. New York: G.P. Putnam's Sons, 1973.

Neumann, Erich. **Depth Psychology and a New Ethic.** London: Hodder and Stoughton, 1969.

Neumann, Erich. **The Great Mother:** An Analysis of the Archetype. London: Routledge and Kegan Paul, 1955.

Neumann, Erich. **The Origins and History of Consciousness.** New York: Pantheon, 1954.

Odajnyk, Walter. **Jung and Politics:** The Political and Social Ideas of Carl Jung. New York: Harper & Row, 1976.

Perry, John Weir. **The Far Side of Madness.** Englewood Cliffs, NJ: Prentice-Hall, 1974.

Perry, John Weir. **Roots of Renewal in Myth and**

Madness: The Meaning of Psychotic Episodes. San Francisco: Jossey-Bass, 1976.

Perry, John Weir. **The Self in Psychotic Process:** Its Symbolization in Schizophrenia. Berkeley: Univ. of CA Press, 1953.

Puer Papers. Irving, TX: Spring Publications, 1978.

Samuels, Andrew. **Jung and the Post-Jungians.** London: Routledge and Kegan Paul, 1985.

Sanford, John A. **The Invisible Partners:** How the Male and Female in Each of Us Affects Our Relationships. New York: Paulist Press, 1980.

The Shaman From Elko: Papers in Honor of Joseph L. Henderson on His Seventy-Fifth Birthday. San Francisco: C.G. Jung Institute of San Francisco, 1978.

Singer, June. **Androgyny:** Toward a New Theory of Sexuality. Garden City, NY: Doubleday, 1976.

Singer, June. **Boundaries of the Soul:** The Practice of Jung's Psychology. Garden City, NY: Doubleday, 1972.

Stein, Murray, ed. **Jungian Analysis.** La Salle, IL: Open Court, 1982.

Stevens, Anthony. **Archetypes:** A Natural History of the Self. New York: Quill, 1983.

Ulanov, Ann Belford. **The Feminine in Jungian Psychology and in Christian Theology.** Evanston: Northwestern Univ. Press, 1971.

Ulanov, Ann and Barry Ulanov. **Religion and the Unconscious.** Philadelphia: Westminster Press, 1975.

Whitmont, Edward C. **The Symbolic Quest:** Basic Concepts of Analytical Psychology. New York: G.P. Putnam's Sons, 1969.

Wickes, Frances Gillespy. **The Inner World of Childhood.** Englewood Cliffs, NJ: Prentice-Hall, 1978.

Wickes, Frances Gillespy. **The Inner World of Choice.** Englewood Cliffs: Prentice-Hall, 1976.

Wickes, Frances Gillespy. **The Inner World of Man.** London: Methuen, 1938.

The **Collected Works** of C.G. Jung:

Vol. 1: **Psychiatric Studies**
Vol. 2: **Experimental Researches**
Vol. 3: **The Psychogenesis of Mental Disease**
Vol. 4: **Freud and Psychoanalysis**
Vol. 5: **Symbols of Transformation**
Vol. 6: **Psychological Types**
Vol. 7: **Two Essays on Analytical Psychology**
Vol. 8: **The Structure and Dynamics of the Psyche**
Vol. 9: Part I: **The Archetypes and the Collective Unconscious**
Vol. 9: Part II: **Aion:** Researches into the Phenomenology of the Self
Vol. 10: **Civilization in Transition**
Vol. 11: **Psychology and Religion: East and West**
Vol. 12: **Psychology and Alchemy**
Vol. 13: **Alchemical Studies**
Vol. 14: **Mysterium Coniunctionis**
Vol. 15: **The Spirit in Man, Art and Literature**
Vol. 16: **The Practice of Psychotherapy**
Vol. 17: **The Development of Personality**
Vol. 18: **The Symbolic Life**
Vol. 19: **General Bibliography of C.G. Jung's Writings**
Vol. 20: **General Index to the Collected Works**
Vol. A: **The Zofingia Lectures**

C.G. Jung: Seminars
    "Fourteen of the seminars which Jung gave between 1925-1942 were recorded in notes by several of his students and later were typed and placed in Jungian libraries for the use of analysts and those in training. Although much of the materials appeared subsequently in the **Collected Works,** the **Seminars** have the freshness of the actual discussions, as well as their informality." (S.F. Jung Library) The **Visions and Dreams Seminars** have been published.

FILMS

"The Houston Films"
Richard Evans conducted four interviews with Jung in Zürich in 1957. The four hours of film have been edited into a two and a half hour version. A transcript can be found in **C.G. Jung Speaking**: Interviews and Encounters, edited by William McGuire and R.F.C. Hull. Princeton: Princeton Univ. Press, 1977.

The "Face To Face" Interview
John Freeman interviewed Jung in 1959 at his home in Küsnacht for BBC's "Face To Face". It is 38 minutes long in black and white. It can be rented from the **C.G. Jung Institute of Chicago** and from **Centerpoint.** For a transcript of the broadcast see **C.G. Jung Speaking.**

"The Story of C.G. Jung"
"This three-part documentary on the life and work of Jung was made on location in Switzerland in 1972 by the BBC. The 90-minute film is narrated by Sir Laurens van der Post.

Part I, "In Search of the Soul", looks at Jung's childhood and student years, his apprenticeship at Zürich's Burghölzli Mental Hospital, his relationship with Sigmund Freud, and the Red Book in which he recorded some of his most intimate and profound paintings and thoughts.

Part II, "67,000 Dreams," shows Jung's work as a psychiatrist, and follows him on his travels. It also visits Bollingen, the private retreat built by Jung on whose stone walls he carved dream figures and mythological motifs.

Part III, "The Mystery that Heals," reveals Jung in old age, examines his views of Christianity and death and discusses the concept of the shadow. Aniela Jaffe and C.A. Meier are also interviewed." (From C.G. Jung Institute of Chicago)

The three 30-minute reels are in color and can be rented from the **Jung Institute of Chicago** and **Centerpoint.**

"The Way of the Dream"

"The Way of the Dream" is a series of 20 half-hour films. Dr. Marie-Louise von Franz interprets dreams and demonstrates how to understand your own dreams. The series are presented under the following topics:

"Introduction: Descent into Dreamland"

"The Foundation": Charting the Unconscious, The Structure of Dreams, The Living Symbol

"Dreams of Men": Our Shadow Knows, The Devouring Mother, Slaying the Dragon, Looking Through the Moon, The Inner Bride, Dreams of a Lifetime

"Dreams of Our Culture": The Ladder to Heaven, The Forgotten Language

"Dreams of Women": Hell Has No Mirrors, The Hanged Man, The Tyrant, Flying Through Roofs, The Inner Guide

"On Relationships": Liberation Of The Heart (Part I), Liberation of The Heart (Part II)

"The Self": The Maker Of Dreams

10 JUNGIAN ANALYSIS
AND TRAINING PROGRAMS

I. Jungian Analysis

The nature of Jungian analysis is described in the two passages below taken from the literature of the C.G. Jung-Institute - Zürich and the **Society of Analytical Psychology** in London. A detailed example of a single analysis can be found in Gerhard Adler's **The Living Symbol,** and more extensive information on analysis and training is in the collection of essays by U.S. analysts entitled **Jungian Analysis,** edited by Murray Stein. Individual analysts can be found through contacting your nearest local or professional group, or consult **The List of Members** of the International Association for Analytical Psychology, Postfach 115, 8042 Zürich, Switzerland. This **Directory** lists analysts by membership in their Jungian professional societies and geographically.

"In its application to psychotherapeutic practice, one of the central and distinguishing features of the Jungian viewpoint is that it sees more in neurotic conflicts and symptoms than merely technical breakdowns of functioning. Thus Jungian therapy is not content with the mere alleviation of symptoms, as seriously as it takes this task. It also seeks to prevent their recurrence by dealing with their deeper causes, which are usually a matter of basic and far-reaching deficiencies: lack of self-knowledge, failure to develop creative potential, doubts about the meaning of life, or absence of a spiritual orientation.

The basic outlook of Jungian psychology makes it possible to offer help in these areas, not in the form of any specific ideology or doctrine of salvation, but through assisting the individual to discover the meaning lying in his own soul. As Jung often stressed, it is finally within the individual, and not on the level of collective social measures, that the problems of our age must be met and the foundations for a healthy democratic society preserved and strengthened." (C.G. Jung-Institute - Zürich)

"Analysis is an individual commitment for both patient and analyst. Although there are certain accepted practices, the conditions of each analysis need to be discussed at the beginning.

Before undertaking the commitment you may be uncertain about the length and frequency of sessions, the duration of the analysis, fees and times. There may be difficulty in finding a suitable analyst. It is not inappropriate to ask for consultation with more than one. Many people are recommended to approach an analyst known to the GP, a counsellor, friend or acquaintance. Others may write to the **Society** to ask for the names of prospective analysts who may have vacancies.

Sessions usually last for 50 minutes and their frequency is from 1-5 times weekly depending on the needs of the individual patient. Fees are negotiated and cannot be quoted here in detail as there is considerable variation. The C.G. Jung Clinic may have vacancies for analysis at reduced fees for those who cannot afford full private fees.

It is impossible to estimate the length of an analysis. Some people need 2-3 years, many require much longer. The process develops its own momentum and many diverse areas of the psyche may need to be explored and revisited on the way." (The Society of Analytical Psychology)

II. Training Programs

Many of the Jungian professional societies have an analyst training program: Zürich, London, New York, Los Angeles, San Francisco, Chicago, Boston and so forth. Detailed program descriptions are available.

The following is a general outline of the basic elements found in most of these programs:

1. Personal Analysis

This is the heart of the program. A certain number of hours of analysis is sometimes required for admission to the training program (e.g. 200 hours for Los Angeles, 150 for New York), and personal analysis continues through the training analysis. Analysis is carried out with both male and female analysts.

"The aim of the training analysis is not simply to learn the techniques of psychotherapy through personal experience, but above all to deepen the future analyst's insight into his own personality structure and his understanding of the manifestations of the unconscious." (C.G. Jung-Institute - Zürich)

2. Formal Study

This takes place in the form of lectures and seminars, and covers the following areas:

I. **Theoretical Foundations:** Origins in psychoanalysis; Comparative theory as a means of differentiation from Freud, Adler, et al.; Relationship between theory and Jung's individuation; Chronological evolution of theory; Present status of theory

II. **Jungian Understanding of Personality and Psychopathology:** Structure and dynamics of the psyche; Psychological types; Complex theory/association experiment; Psychopathology - diagnosis, comparative theory of neurosis, theory of psychosis, defense mechanisms, symptomatology, etc.; Individuation process

III. **The Practice of Jungian Analysis:** Transference/countertransference theory and management; Frame or container issues; Phases of analysis; The appropriate utilization of imaginal techniques

IV. **Techniques for Activation and Interpretation of the Unconscious:** Dream theory and interpretation; Active imagination; Sand tray; Picture interpretation; Amplification; Reductive and synthetic interpretation

V. **Archetypal Material:** Mythology; Fairy tales and folklore; Comparative religion; Ethnology; Anthropology (C.G. Jung Institute of Chicago)

3. The Control Stage
Practical supervised experience in doing Jungian analysis, case colloquia and clinic experience

4. An examination in the subject matter of analytical psychology and the writing of a thesis

5. Admission requirements
They vary considerably, from an M.D. or a degree in clinical psychology with clinic experience (with exceptions made) to the greater latitude at the Jung Institute of Zürich:
"The **Zürich Institute** holds firmly to its policy of considering applicants from all academic backgrounds and professions. Three decades of experience with this policy have shown that representatives of other disciplines (philosophy, literature, law, the natural sciences, etc.) can also have the qualities needed to become gifted psychotherapists. Moreover, the **Institute** believes, with Jung, that this openness to the full gamut of human experience enriches analytical psychology as a science and, above all, is essential for a psychotherapy capable of doing justice to the needs of the whole human being. Thus the **Institute** remains a relatively unique place in this age of specialization, where a lively exchange is continually in progress between people of the most diverse back-

grounds and viewpoints." (C.G. Jung Institute - Zür-ich)

Facts about the **Zürich Training Program:**
The minimal time in the Zürich program is 3 years, and the average is 4 1/2 years

"Almost two-thirds of the students in training come from outside Switzerland. More than 30 nation-alities are represented, with the largest contingents being from the USA, Germany, Italy, Great Britain, Canada, Brazil and Japan.

The entire training program is offered in German and English, and selected courses in Italian and French.

There are presently over 300 students in training, and over 100 Jungian analysts (as well as specialists from other fields) contributing to the training pro-gram in various capacities.

More than 250 graduates of the **Institute** are now practicing on 4 continents, and around 30 new Jung-ian analysts receive their diplomas each year.

Around 80 lecture courses, seminars, and case colloquia - representing over 700 hours of instruction - are offered each semester."

INDEX TO LISTINGS

ST. JOHN OF THE CROSS
AND DR. C. G. JUNG

CHRISTIAN MYSTICISM
IN THE LIGHT OF
JUNGIAN PSYCHOLOGY

BY JAMES ARRAJ

Many current attempts to revitalize the life of prayer are inspired by either the writings of St. John of the Cross or the psychology of Dr. C. G. Jung. Both are excellent choices. Even better would be a program of renewal under their joint inspiration.

Yet such a program faces three serious challenges: theological misgivings about the compatibility of Jung's psychology with Christian belief, long-standing misinterpretations of St. John's doctrine on contemplation, and the need to clarify the relationship between Jung's process of individuation and contemplation.

Parts I and II are devoted to resolving these first two problems, while Part III gives a practical demonstration of the relationship between individuation and contemplation in St. John's life and writings and in a variety of contemporary spiritual problems.

Let me put it more concretely. I am enthusiastic about the prospect of using Jung and St. John as practical guides in the interior life. But when this enthusiasm begins to run away with me I see Victor White deep in conversation with Jung in the tower at Bollingen and their subsequent estrangement. Or I see Juan Falconi and Antonio Rojas in the Madrid of the late 1620's evoking the name of John of the Cross with the best of intentions to fuel a popular enthusiasm for contemplation, yet paving the road that led to a distrust of mysticism that has lingered to our own day.

Although these problems are serious and will force us to take a difficult journey through the thickets of epistemology and the history of spiritual life in the 17th century, I believe they are surmountable and will help lay foundations for a renewal of the life of prayer and a practical science of spiritual direction.

FROM THE INTRODUCTION

200 pages, 5 1/2 x 8 1/2, paperback original, index, bibliography, notes, ISBN 0-914073-02-8, $11.95.

THE TREASURES OF SIMPLE LIVING

A FAMILY'S SEARCH FOR A SIMPLER AND MORE MEANINGFUL LIFE IN THE MIDDLE OF A FOREST

by TYRA ARRAJ with JAMES ARRAJ

Our future was set out for us: full-time jobs, mortgage payments for the next 20 years, and retirement at 65. Our children would go to school and we would see them as much as our busy schedules allowed. But such a future held no attraction for us. So we packed up, left it all behind and drove into the unknown.

Our journey took us beyond the electric lines, telephone, paved roads and television. We built our own house, grew salads year-round in a solar greenhouse and taught our children at home, all in the midst of a forest where the nearest neighbors are wild animals and the snow gets four feet deep.

The inconveniences were soon forgotten in the joys of living under our own roof, watching our children blossom and discovering abilities we never knew we had. The simplicity took away economic pressures and gave us time to search for life's deeper meanings.

PART I explains why we left the city, how we solved the problem of earning a living and what we went through once we bought a piece of land in the middle of a forest. Read about: the rat race, searching for land, house-building, alternative utilities, a greenhouse-bioshelter, tofu and tempeh, life without a television and home school.

PART II tells about the treasures we found in our simple life, why our experiment paid us back a thousand-fold, and the dream of a bioshelter community.

PART III describes common obstacles to creating a new lifestyle closer to nature, and some important skills like crafts, economic basics, orthomolecular medicine, and human differences, that helped us along the way.

PART IV is a **Resource Guide** for those who might like to begin their own adventure in simple living, including books and organizations on the subjects covered in the first three sections.

FROM THE INTRODUCTION

216 pages, 5 1/2 x 8 1/2, paperback original, resource guide, 14 line drawings, index
ISBN 0-914073-04-4, $11.95.

COMING SOON:

TRACKING THE ELUSIVE HUMAN

A GUIDE TO
C.G. JUNG'S PSYCHOLOGICAL TYPES,
WILLIAM SHELDON'S BODY TYPES
AND THEIR INTEGRATION

by TYRA ARRAJ and JAMES ARRAJ

This extensive, detailed and practical book includes:

PART I
descriptions of the basic elements of Jung's typology and the eight basic types
the principles that govern type development
types in daily life
types and falling in love, marriage and children
descriptions of Sheldon's body and temperament types and how they can be developed
the integration of these two typologies

PART II includes detailed discussions of:
the origins of Jung's psychological types
typology since Jung
new developments
William Sheldon's life and work
an evaluation of the criticisms that surrounded his work
the problems of creating an integrated typology
the search for a biochemical typology
and whether there is a relationship between typology and modern neuroscience and genetics

large bibliography, quizzes, illustrations

ORDER FORM

Please send me:

_____copy(s) of A Jungian Psychology Resource Guide
    at $11.95 each.

_____copy(s) of St. John of the Cross and Dr. C.G.
    Jung at $11.95 each.

_____copy(s) of The Treasures of Simple Living at
    $11.95 each.

_____information on Tracking the Elusive Human.

Add $1.00 for the first book and $.50 for each
additional book. Enclosed is my check/money order
for $_____.

NAME_____

STREET_____

CITY_____STATE_____ZIP_____

Send to: TOOLS FOR INNER GROWTH
              Box 520
              Chiloquin, OR 97624

ORDER FORM

Please send me:

_____copy(s) of A Jungian Psychology Resource Guide
    at $11.95 each.

_____copy(s) of St. John of the Cross and Dr. C.G.
    Jung at $11.95 each.

_____copy(s) of The Treasures of Simple Living at
    $11.95 each.

_____information on Tracking the Elusive Human.

Add $1.00 for the first book and $.50 for each
additional book. Enclosed is my check/money order
for $_____.

NAME_____

STREET_____

CITY_____STATE_____ZIP_____

Send to: TOOLS FOR INNER GROWTH
              Box 520
              Chiloquin, OR 97624

ORDER FORM

Please send me:

_____copy(s) of A Jungian Psychology Resource Guide at $11.95 each.

_____copy(s) of St. John of the Cross and Dr. C.G. Jung at $11.95 each.

_____copy(s) of The Treasures of Simple Living at $11.95 each.

_____information on Tracking the Elusive Human.

Add $1.00 for the first book and $.50 for each additional book. Enclosed is my check/money order for $_____.

NAME_____

STREET_____

CITY_____STATE_____ZIP_____

Send to: TOOLS FOR INNER GROWTH
             Box 520
             Chiloquin, OR 97624

ORDER FORM

Please send me:

_____copy(s) of A Jungian Psychology Resource Guide at $11.95 each.

_____copy(s) of St. John of the Cross and Dr. C.G. Jung at $11.95 each.

_____copy(s) of The Treasures of Simple Living at $11.95 each.

_____information on Tracking the Elusive Human.

Add $1.00 for the first book and $.50 for each additional book. Enclosed is my check/money order for $_____.

NAME_____

STREET_____

CITY_____STATE_____ZIP_____

Send to: TOOLS FOR INNER GROWTH
             Box 520
             Chiloquin, OR 97624